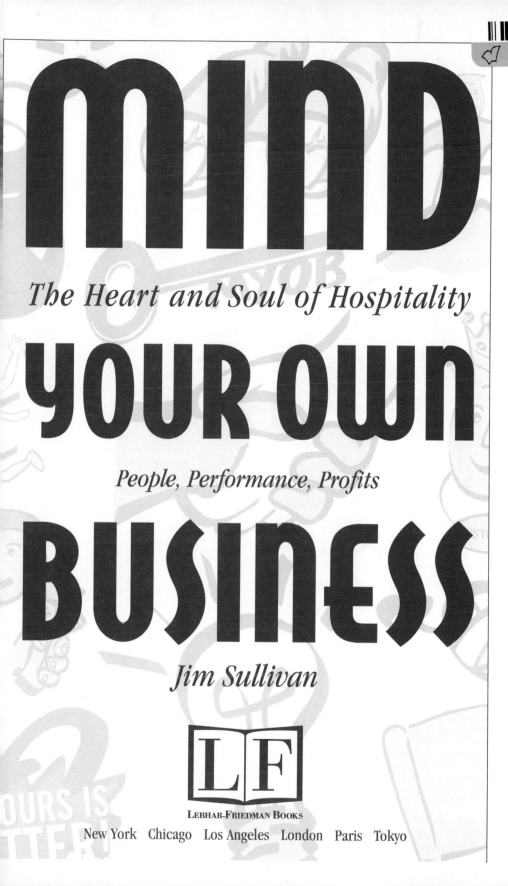

MIND

The Heart and Soul of Hospitality

YOUR OWN

People, Performance, Profits

BUSINESS

Jim Sullivan

LF

LEBHAR-FRIEDMAN BOOKS

New York   Chicago   Los Angeles   London   Paris   Tokyo

To Richards and the Bean

Lebhar-Friedman Books
425 Park Avenue
New York, NY 10022

Copyright © 1999 Jim Sullivan

Published by Lebhar-Friedman Books
Lebhar-Friedman Books is a company of Lebhar-Friedman Inc.

Printed in the United States of America

Library of Congress Cataloging-in-Publication Data
Sullivan, Jim. 1952-
    Mind your own business : managing the heart and soul of
hospitality : people, performance, profits / Jim Sullivan.
            p.   cm.
     ISBN 0-86730-766-8
     1. Restaurant Management.   I. Title.
 TX911.3.M27S85   1999
 647.95'068--dc2I   99-23635
                                                           CIP

Cover design, illustration and book layout:
CLICK! Visuals
(800) 490-3210, www.clickvisuals.com

Visit our Web site at lfbooks.com

CONTENTS

SEARCHING FOR THE HEART AND SOUL OF HOSPITALITY

My family and I recently moved from Denver to the town of Grand Chute in beautiful northeast Wisconsin. You're pretty much in dairy country in these here parts. It's the kind of place where if baby Superman crash-landed, the townspeople would raise him to be a cheese farmer. But my weekly travels and our tens of thousands of customers keep me very much in daily touch with the turbo-changing world of hospitality in the 21st Century. It's here in Grand Chute that I've collected and combined the absolute best and newest service, sales, marketing and team-building performance practices into what has become Mind Your Own Business, the book.

Successful companies like American Express, Walt Disney Company, Coca-Cola, TGI Friday's, McDonald's, Kroger, Holiday Inns Worldwide, Starbucks, Dayton/Hudson Stores, Applebee's and thousands of others worldwide have been using my service and sales training programs for the last decade. The hundreds of consulting opportunities and thousands of seminars I've led have given me a unique opportunity to both teach and learn. This book therefore, is a collaborative project between me and everyone I have the pleasure of working with, and I would be seriously remiss in not thanking the following colleagues, clients and friends for their collective mentoring, inspiration and support:

Mary Adolf	David Aisenstat	Scott Allmendinger	Bill Anton
Geoff Bailey	Ted Balestreri	Ned Barker	Todd Barnum
Bob Basham	Michael Bartlett	Frank Belatti	Debi Beneditti
Ken Blanchard	Annette Boulay	Ken Boulay	Ralph Brennan
Norman Brinker	Doug Brooks	Jim Buelt	Greg Burns

Steve Burd
Mike Cardello
John Cleese
Ken Cole
Mark Cummins
Stan Dickman
Len Dreyer
Bob Fletcher
Tim Gannon
Dan Gordon
Tim Hammonds
Joe Hoff
John Keener
Kevin Knee
Joe Lee
Bill Lindig
Roz Mallet
Bernie McGorry
Rich Melman
Dave Miller
Bill Morgan
Stan Novack
Stewart Owens
Tom Peters
Tom Rector
Ed Rensi
Skip Sack
Andy Seymor
Gary Sobkowiak
Joe Stubbs
Kevin Todd
Cheryl Tyler
Jack Welch

August Busch IV
Mike Charlton
Lee Cockcrell
Buster Corley
John Daschler
Fred DiMicco
Steve Ells
Scott Follett
Dick Gaven
Alan Gould
Steve Hester
Cliff Hudson
Bill Kimpton
Wayne Kolberg
Emeril Lagasse
Beth Lorenzini
Stuart Mann
Bill McLaughlin
Ferdinand Metz
Hala Moddelmog
Peter Morton
David Novak
Ron Paul
Steve Phillips
Harry Riegert
Bill Reynolds
Mike Sansolo
Eddie Sheldrake
Jeremy Spencer
R.P. Sullivan
Kuni Toyoda
Nick Valenti
Lloyd M. Wirshba

Steve Caldeira
Carol Christison
Doug Coen
Tom Costello
Frank Day
Jim Doherty
Mike Feeney
Shannon Foust
Don Goetz
Kathy Granquist
Bill Higgins
Tony Hughes
Gerry Kinsella
Ellen Koteff
Randy Lett
Vern Lusbey
Ron McDougal
Drew McMillen
Joe Micatrotto
Ernie Monschein
Lee Nichols
Larry Oberkfell
Caroline Perkins
Joseph Pichler
Kelli Rehder
Dick Rivera
T.J. Schier
Jon Sleik
Frank Steed
Rick Sullivan
Jackie Trujillo
Tom Walters
Kathleen Wood

Loret Carbone
Mark Christopher
Carla Cooper
Craig Culver
Mike DeLuca
Wally Doolin
Tillman Fertitta
Ted Fowler
Geoff Golson
Larry Griewisch
Lloyd Hill
Matt Jones
Malcolm Knapp
Toni Kottom
Mike Licata
Ken Madison
Bill McHugh
John McQueeny
Cameron Mitchell
Ellen Moore
Drew Nieporent
Tim O'Byrne
Roberta Perry
Robert Plotkin
Ernie Renaud
Tim Ryan
Howard Schultz
Mike Snyder
Julia Stewart
Chris Sullivan
Steve Tyink
Rick Van Warner
Dave Young

This book is about a simple premise: that the workplace should be both recognized and managed as a gathering of people and ideas working together toward profitability—not just a financial machine staffed by "human capital" to make a profit. It's a lot about heart. And all about soul.

My intention is to inform, educate, innovate and have fun. So let's get it on. In summary? Never forget that there are two basic strategies for success in business: One, never reveal all you know.

PEOPLE
PERFORMANCE
PROFITS

> *"There are two ways of spreading light: To be the candle or the mirror that reflects it."*
>
> -Edith Wharton, Novelist

Over 3,000 business books are published each year in the United States. Many of us buy most of them hoping to find that one idea, that one inspirational message, that one creative trick, tip, or technique that will jump-start our performance and send profits soaring. Me too. But I'll be the first to admit that you can no more run a better business just by reading a book than you can become an automobile by sleeping in a garage. What were once good ideas quickly become cliches in the turbo-charged business world. Just mention the words "excellence," "re-engineering," "habits," "soup," or "giants within" to most business owners, and they'll take off quicker than Ted Kennedy at an O'Doul's kegger.

So I can't promise you "excellence," but I will deliver the best ideas I can find. I can't change your "habits," but I'll detail the most effective profitability behavior in the business. I can't bring "soup" for your soul, but I can bring heart to your team's performance and better profits to your bottom line. I can't even really save you time, but I promise I won't waste your money. I also promise to use statistics sparingly, the same way a drunk uses a lamp post—not for illumination but support. I can't guarantee you'll go straight to Successville, but I will draw the road map. The ideas detailed in this book are effective because they're used every day in thousands of successful

restaurants, supermarkets, hotels, and retail stores worldwide. As different as those industries are, they all have one product in common: Hospitality. The word "service" is so overpromised and underdelivered that it has nearly lost its meaning and value in today's business world. I believe that the word hospitality, not service, conjures up a more accurate description of the feeling we're trying to transfer to our customers…and employees.

Service is "given." Hospitality is felt.

Service has become a commodity. Hospitality still can be customized and help you attract new customers and employees.

Service is a process. Hospitality is heart and soul.

Service is dead. Long live *Chispa!*
(*Chispa!* means "Electric hospitality"–more on that later.)

I've researched and documented the creative performance strategies of hundreds of successful restaurant, retail, hotel, and supermarket companies worldwide. This is their story, these are their profitability practices, and this is my guarantee: all killer, no filler. This book is based on today's workplace realities, the "faster-harder-smarter-more," business world we all work in. Live it or live with it.

Unlike most "consultants" who write business books, I am still in the hospitality business every day, maybe just as you are. Sure, I have those days when I look around at the multiple fires that need tending and ask myself, "Where am I going, and what am I doing in this handbasket?" But the feeling passes quicker than a cappuccino burrito, and I'm left with that unique combination of wonderment, exhaustion, and exhilaration that typifies a Day in the Life of a hospitality pro.

SERVICE is "given." Hospitality is felt.

SERVICE has become a commodity.

HOSPITALITY can still be customized and help you attract new customers and employees.

SERVICE is a process. Hospitality is heart and soul.

SERVICE is "dead." Long live CHISPA ! ("electric hospitality")

7

Mind Your Own Business (MYOB) is focused on members of the hospitality business, whom I define as operators or employees of restaurants, hotels, retail stores, or supermarkets, chain or independents, big or small. And for those impatient readers already glancing at your watch, I'll present my *Cliff's Notes* version of MYOB right up front. I agree with and will address the following philosophies– read 'em and reap:

Any dope with a checkbook can buy a business. It's what you do afterward that matters.

One good definition of insanity is to keep doing the same things over and over again and expect different results.

The problem is never how to get new and innovative ideas into your mind, but how to get the old ones out.

Excellent companies don't believe in excellence– only in constant improvement, constant change, and constant training.

The speed of the leader determines the rate of the pack.

Owning a business is *not* the functional equivalent of having no boss. We don't own our business; the customer does. We work for our customers because if we don't satisfy them, somebody else will. And when we're done working for the customer, we work for our employees.

If Patrick Henry thought taxation without representation was bad, he should see it with representation.

There is no labor crisis. It's a turnover crisis. Focus your energies on retaining your good people, and you won't have to worry about finding new ones.

EMPLOYEES' CREED:
FOR EVERY DUMB
SYSTEM YOU CREATE
THAT WE DON'T LIKE,
WE WILL CREATE
AN EQUAL AND
OPPOSITE SYSTEM.

8

Man must sit for very long time with mouth open before roast duck fly in.

School is never out for the pro.

When someone gets something for nothing, someone else gets nothing for something.

The difference between business reality and fiction is simple: Fiction has to make sense.

Underpromise and overdeliver.

Jim Sullivan's "Extinction" theory: Good work that goes unacknowledged gradually will **disappear**.

The two most common elements in the universe are hydrogen and stupidity. Don't ever assume you've got it all figured out, because eventually your customers or competitors will outfigure you. You made it idiot proof? Somebody will make a better idiot.

All work is teamwork.

If you torture numbers they'll confess to anything. Use your P&L as a compass, but not as the bottom line in all decision-making.

Your two biggest challenges? Retaining the best people, and improving their productivity.

Don't be a corporate weenie.

One good definition of insanity is to keep doing the same things over and over again and expect different results.

9

Don't ever practice on the customer. Effective employee performance is your fiercest weapon and biggest competitive edge in the battle for the customer. No train, no gain.

What isn't tried won't work.

The current business mantra of "grow or die" should be modified to "grow profitably or don't grow at all."

Our real bottom line is not how much we get from our customers, it's how much they get from us.

The customer is not always right. That implies that in every situation, the employee is always wrong. The customer is not always right, but is always the customer–and it's alright for the customer to be wrong.

You didn't learn to ride a bike in a seminar. Treat learning as a process, not an "event." Educate daily. Make learning fun, experiential, and interactive. What we learn with pleasure, we never forget.

It is better to be approximately right than to be precisely wrong.

Nothing is new except what's been forgotten.

If you cannot win, make the person in front of you set the record.

Always imitate the behavior of winners when you lose.

Knowledge, not time, is money.

Know the Law of Probability Dispersal: Whatever it is that hits the fan will not be evenly distributed.

10

Support your community. Creating "social profit" is critical to both acquiring customers and retaining good employees.

Different is not always better, but better is always different. I don't know the key to success, but the key to failure is trying to please everybody.

Last but not least, here is the best piece of advice I could give for running a successful hospitality operation:

THE MOST POWERFUL WEAPON ON EARTH IS THE HUMAN SOUL ON FIRE.

If your employees and customers are anything like ours, they smell complacency and inertia. Then they go somewhere else. They want to work for or patronize the inspired company or leader that lights the way with a blowtorch, rather than a handful of uninspired, heartless managers holding candles. Passion persuades.

If you're no longer driven, find a new way to steer your business. If you're no longer passionate, rediscover the romance of your profession. If you've lost the spark, let the sheer *joie de vivre* of this business relight your fire. If you've tried and tried but just can't step up to the plate anymore, that's OK. You're never a loser until you quit trying.

That's what *Mind Your Own Business* is all about: igniting blowtorches, creating or re-discovering the passion and purpose, overturning myths that inhibit performance, taking care of your people, and most important, making your customers lives more stress-free and your employee's jobs more meaningful.

Passion persuades.

The best managers are energy managers.

Illuminate the workplace with a blowtorch, don't carry a candle.

Mind Your Own Business is about seeking the heart and soul of hospitality–and then defining it in ways that make your customers return, your employees happier, and your bottom line bigger. It's about focusing on creating strong emotional connections with people first, and then improving performance and profitability. It's about the basics, the new customer rules, how to post a winning P&L and, ultimately, it's about execution. Every day, every shift, 24/7-type execution. After all, words are words, explanations are explanations, promises are promises–but only performance is reality. Or, in the inimitable words of former major league pitcher Johnny Sain: "Don't tell me about the labor pains; show me the baby!"

I suggest a cafeteria-style approach to *Mind Your Own Business*: Pick and choose the ideas that are most relevant to your operation, and leave the ones you don't care for. In other words, try it if you like it, ditch it if you don't. Every idea here is not new or undiscovered. But each one is practical and guaranteed effective. So, as you begin reading and your brain interrupts with IKTA (I Know That Already), challenge yourself right back with BAIDI (But Am I Doing It?).

IKTA vs. BAIDI

(I Know That Already
But Am I Doing It?)

The Japanese have a great word called *shoshin,* which means "beginner's mind." Author Shunryu Suzuki explains it thusly: "This does not mean a closed mind, but actually an empty mind and a ready mind. If your mind is empty, it

is always ready for anything. It is open to everything. In the beginner's mind, there are many possibilities; in the expert's mind there are few." Think like a beginner, not an expert, when reading through this book. Suspend what you know and empty–don't open–your mind to the ideas in each chapter.

Who Am I To Tell You What To Do?

"The function of the expert is not to be more right than other people, but to be wrong for more sophisticated reasons." –Brett Gosse, supermarket executive.

I'll be the first to admit that I probably cannot teach you anything. After all, in college I graduated in the part of the class that made the top half possible. And while I've been labeled an "expert" in the areas of improving service and increasing sales, I take the label with the appropriate grain of salt. You can't always go by expert opinion. A turkey, if you ask a turkey, should be stuffed with grasshoppers, grit, and worms, right? So don't look for expert advice from me; just take the enclosed practical ideas and *execute* expertness in your own business. As Ben Franklin observed: *"Well done is better than well said."*

MYOB is all about igniting purpose and passion in the marketplace. So let's get it on. I see managing the heart and soul of hospitality as four distinct categories:

Be good at what you do.
Be good at what the customer wants.
Be good at what the employee needs.
Be good to yourself.

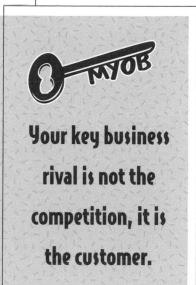

Your key business rival is not the competition, it is the customer.

MARKETING

New! OURS IS BETTER!

> **I**f you can convince your customers to tattoo your name on their chests, they probably will not shift brands." —Robert W. Hall on customer loyalty to Harley-Davidson motorcycles

What if someone knocked on your door tomorrow morning and said, *"I want to pay for your mortgage, car, kid's tuition, weekly groceries, and the next 10 vacations?"*

How would you treat that person?

I don't know about you, but I'd be jumping off my keister and dusting off a special spot on the old Lazyboy™ recliner for the kindly stranger. Well, guess what? Someone does pay for our house, holidays, transportation, and tuition every day in our businesses.

And that person is called The Customer.

Cherish your customers. Obsess about them. Worry about them. Jealously guard them from the competition. Serve them. And serve them well. The one thing all businesses need more than an electronic database or even higher sales is more customers. This chapter will detail myriad ways to get more customers' feet on the floor and more keisters in the seats.

"The most expensive thing in a restaurant is an empty chair."

– Jack Kriendler, founder, The "21 Club", NYC

Two common reasons for failing at business are not knowing that you're competing in the first place, and not knowing with whom you're competing. In this chapter we'll focus on cost-effective and revenue-generating ways to gain more customers at the competition's expense.

A business has two kinds of customers:

- New
- Existing

Which of the two has the most theoretical value, and which is the most profitable to you *right now*? Always market to the greatest share of opportunity. But before you go out and "Ralph Kramden" a lot of crazy ways to get new customers in your door, make sure that your current customers are both being served and sold to fully. Sales managers call it "account penetration." That may sound like a crude way to refer to a customer, but the point is that you must first fully build business with present customers as you try to fill the pipeline with new ones. Prioritize your market strategy accordingly.

Remember that your new and existing customers are also broken down into:

- External customers (paying patrons who walk through the front door) and
- Internal customers (employees and vendors who walk through the back door)

I'm no sculptor, but you can carve this one in stone: The way you treat your employees determines how they'll treat your customers. In this chapter we'll examine cost-effective marketing ideas that help us build traffic. In the next chapter we'll detail effective service tactics that make

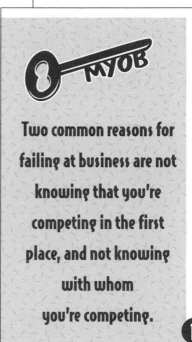

Two common reasons for failing at business are not knowing that you're competing in the first place, and not knowing with whom you're competing.

15

for happy external and internal customers and improved profitability. So let's begin with the basics: creative ways to get customers in the door of our store since the most expensive thing in any business is–an empty store.

Grass Roots Creative Marketing 101

In his book *Selling With Service*, Phil Wexler says that *the function of a business is to acquire and maintain customers. The goal is to make money.* He suggests we focus on the former and the latter will take care of itself. I tend to agree, but I can recall plenty of times when we were plenty full with customers (we attained our function), but we lost money (missing the goal) because of waste, breakage, attitudes, and a prolific lack of upselling. Still, the one thing all businesses need more than a facelift, menu makeover, or sexy software, is new customers. So here's a list of some of my favorite cost-effective and street-savvy marketing techniques:

- **Fishbowls.** This tried but true method for soliciting new or repeat business is a restaurant classic and works equally well in a supermarket deli. Place a fishbowl by your front door or on your deli case with a sign that says, "Please drop in your business card and/or e-mail address for a weekly drawing for a free lunch (or dinner) for two. Add your birthdate for a special gift." The drawing doesn't have to be random. Carefully review each card before choosing a winner, and ask yourself this question: "Which person here is most likely to bring me the most business?" When you spot the card from a decision-maker with a lot of employees within a short drive of your restaurant, declare a winner, and make that call! That free lunch pays for itself many times over. Now draw a truly random card and feel better about the process. Put all the names, businesses, and birthdays from the cards that didn't "win" into your database software for your seasonal, special occasion and email lists, and start collecting again for next week's winner.

- **Write five handwritten thank-you notes a day.**
You know you don't have time to write five handwritten thank-you notes each day and so do your customers. That's why they'll appreciate it so much. In this age of "faster-harder-smarter-more," your customers will appreciate the greatest gift you can give–your time–with the thoughtfulness of hand-penned note. Want to add even more flair to the gesture? Enclose a quick-pick Lotto ticket for the next drawing and remark how customers are million-dollar assets to your business. You've got a database. Use it.

- **Market to your invisible customers.** Distributor sales reps, delivery people, meter readers, postal workers, and vending-machine stockers are all potential customers, so be sure to treat those folks with courtesy and respect. Offer gift certificates or free appetizer coupons to encourage them to dine with you or patronize your takeout business. P.S. Those folks are also keen observers of how safely you handle your food behind the scenes.

- **"Steal" the best ideas.** The best business owners are shameless "thieves" in terms of "borrowing" good

Place laminated "to go" menus in every hotel room within a 5 mile radius. Have plastic static clings made of your logo and phone number and put them on every hotel television. Work the hotel bartenders, not just the concierge, to recommend your restaurant to guests.

ideas. Pay attention to what other restaurants, bars, nightclubs, supermarkets, retail stores are doing in the marketplace and encourage your staff to collect information/flyers, etc. and share it with you. After all, they go out to more bars, restaurants, grocery stores, nightclubs, and other businesses collectively in a month than you could in an entire year. Encourage them to note and share unique promotions, and collect flyers or ads. Especially encourage them to ask their friends or family that work at other restaurants or stores about what their employers are doing internally to improve service, increase sales, or stage effective employee contests and rewards. Then adapt, innovate, and improve on those ideas.

- **Deliver free food to morning or afternoon drive-time DJs:** Want your food quality broadcast around the area without having to buy expensive radio ads? Get up early and prepare some of your signature items, grab a couple of T-shirts and hats, if you sell them, and take them to the local radio station drive-time disc jockeys. It can pay off with tons of free publicity. Pick your best-looking and most articulate employees, and dress them up neatly in your restaurant's logo-ed clothing. The DJs are appreciative, always dig in right away, and usually wax poetic about the great food–and your operation–to their tens of thousands of listeners in the key drive-time periods.

18

- **Market to your acquaintances.** Studies show that the average person knows nearly 250 people either directly or indirectly. What if we could inspire or motivate each of our employees and managers to bring in just three of their 250 acquaintances as new customers? If you employ 30 people, that's another 90 new customers. If your average transaction is $10 per person, and customers tend to patronize you, say, 10 times a year, that's another $9,000 in higher gross sales from a referral of just three people from each employee. What if you have 100 employees, and they each bring in three new customers? Let's see, my calculator's here somewhere... ah, there it is: that's $30,000 in new business. And if each of these new customers just told one of *their* friends...well, I think you get my drift.

Here's how to make it work in a restaurant, hotel, or supermarket deli: Have employees hand out special cards with their names on them. Each card is good for one free appetizer, sandwich, dessert, or beverage. But wait, don't stop there, because if you've tried this idea in the past, you know that the results can be disappointing (people redeem the coupons for the free item but purchase little–or nothing–else.) Why? You overlooked the most important step. Make sure that you record and post the total check average or purchase of each redeemed card on a list next to each employee's name. Reward the team members whose customers had the highest total purchases among the cards redeemed, not just the person who had the most cards redeemed. Your staff may be motivated to suggestively sell more to the card recipients during their "free" visit.

www.yourbiz.com

Be Cyber Savvy

Don't settle for the number of "hits" you get at your website. Your objective is to gather names, addresses, and birthdays, not "website visits." Entice customers to register at your website with a 10% off coupon or a free appetizer offer.

- **Web-based marketing.** The Internet has become more sophisticated relative to business and personal website design, and you need to be cyber-savvy to draw attention to yours. The best rule of thumb I can suggest is to design your website from the customer's point-of-view. Keep it visual, fun, and resist the urge to thump your chest about how the company began, your mission statement, the number of people you serve and zzzzz! A good way to focus on the customer design-wise is to prominently feature FAQ (Frequently Asked Questions) about your company. That forces you to think from the customer's perspective and also tends to engage and involve the customer more quickly. Next, try to collect as many e-mail addresses from your customers as you can. Then send out occasional e-mails that inform the customers about upcoming promotions and specials. Heck, why not turn that promo e-mail into a coupon, informing the reader that if they bring that e-mail in to your restaurant or business, they'll get 10 percent off their bill. Or why not feature a coupon on your website that can be downloaded as a "special thanks to our Internet customers," Try it, you've got little to lose. The other basics relative to designing an effective website? Contact all the relevant search engines to get your website listed, respond to all e-mail within 24 hours, keep your site current and updated, and put your e-mail address in all ads, business cards, brochures, stationery, and point-of-sale.

- **"Buy a drink for a friend" sign.** Post a chalkboard behind the bar that encourages patrons to buy a drink or an appetizer for a friend who isn't there. Then write the customer's name and the item waiting for them on the chalkboard legibly with colored chalk. All your other customers see it as they visit the bar, and many impulsively will buy a drink or appetizer for someone they know who isn't there. When the new customer comes in and "cashes in," erase the name from the chalkboard. Obviously, the drink buyer pays in advance and encourages the friend to visit your restaurant/bar ASAP. This could be adapted to a supermarket deli, too.

- **Make charitable events win-win.** If a local group is looking to hold a fund-raising dinner, why not volunteer your restaurant? You donate 25 to 50 percent of the proceeds to the charity, they do all the marketing and word-of-mouth. Be sure you distribute gift certificates or "buy-one-get-one" lunch coupons to all the charity diners to promote repeat business.

The two magic words of target marketing are: "unfulfilled needs."

- **Walking billboards.** To extend your brand further into the marketplace, consider selling logo merchandise—mugs, T-shirts, hats, shoes, glasses, pins, etc.—from your operation. It extends your product line without increasing labor costs. Russ Adams, owner of the Strongbow Inn in Valparaiso, Indiana has this to say about merchandise: "The margin's good, it's cheap advertising, and you don't have to refrigerate them." What restaurateur doesn't envy the merchandise lines and sales at Hard Rock Cafe? We've been extremely successful selling T-shirts and hats at our restaurants over the years, and here are a few hints on how to make it work for you:

   Determine a fair price for your T-shirts or hats. Now add a dollar more. Give that dollar as a commission to employees who sell a shirt or hat.

   Prominently display the name of your city on the shirt or hat. That dramatically improves its appeal as a souvenir and collectible.

   Display your shirts and hats prominently throughout the restaurant and bar. Post the price large and legibly on each item to improve impulse buying.

   Offer a fun incentive to encourage your customers to wear your logo T-shirts as much as possible when they travel. Post pictures in your restaurant of customers wearing your T-shirts in front of famous landmarks or signs as they travel. For instance, shots in front of the Eiffel Tower, the pyramids, Disneyland, Wrigley Field, and so on. Put up a sign near the photos explaining that you want more shots for the "Wall of Fame." Tell your customers to bring in the pictures, and then write the guests names prominently on the photo and post it on the wall. You'll be amazed how many people will come in for dinner or drinks with their friends just to show off the pictures. Plus, it just generally adds fun and flair to a blank wall. Try it. It works.

- **Reward frequent buyers with double dip on slower days.** If you have a frequent shopper or frequent diner program that awards points to customers for each dollar they spend, good for you. Then take a tip from the Chart House Restaurants: To encourage more patronage at slower times, the chain offers double points for their frequent shoppers program on Monday nights to build traffic on this historically slow night for restaurateurs.

23

- **Own a golf tournament.** As a business owner you are bombarded with dozens of requests daily to support charities, each promising "a lot" of business in return. Golf tournaments are a favorite, but what do you really get for sponsoring a hole for $1,000? Good will? Maybe. More business? Possibly. But I'd like to suggest a better way based on an idea I heard from John Keener, owner of The Charleston Crab House restaurant group in South Carolina. He suggests sponsoring a "hole-in-one" contest on a par three for $10,000 instead of the $1,000 hole sponsorship. Sound crazy? Well, John ponies up about $500 for hole-in-one insurance, and gets all the publicity for 50 percent of what his fellow sponsors are paying to generically sponsor one of the other holes.

"Anyone who thinks you're too small to be effective has never been in bed with a mosquito."

—Anita Ruddick, founder of The Body Shop

- **Assemble an internal marketing task force.** Who needs an expensive marketing consultant when you could assemble a task force of employees from different departments to execute commando marketing tactics in your area? A leader should be chosen, and once a month the group should convene for 60 minutes to share new ideas and brainstorm cost-effective ways for you to bring in more customers. Don't judge or dismiss any ideas in front of the group. In fact, the wackier the idea, the better it might be. We've done this with great success at our restaurants for the last 14 years, and here's probably the best idea that has paid off time and time again:

- **Take out your local Yellow Pages.** Turn at random to any section. Let's say it's "Veterinarians." Now brainstorm all of the professions or businesses in your local marketplace that relate to vets. A partial list might include:

Dog Breeders	Pet groomers
Riding clubs	Kennels
Pet trainers	Dog or Horse tracks
Pet stores	Dog/Cat/Horse clubs
Dude ranches	ASPCA

That's a list of at least nine areas of opportunity to which you can market. Ask your assembled task force the following questions: Do the local dog clubs, riding clubs, or groomers go out to eat and drink individually or as a group? Do they have meetings? Awards banquets? Who's the contact person? When are the meetings held?

I think you can see where I'm going here. The next step obviously is to assign two people to be the team leaders to contact the decision-makers in each group and solicit their business for your restaurant or deli. Letters of invitation filled with free appetizer coupons good only on one of your slower nights work best. We go a step further by inviting those groups into our restaurants between 5 PM and 7 PM on a Tuesday or Wednesday evening for a free appetizer buffet set up with their group's name on it in an area near the bar. The key is not to isolate the group away from the bar area. They receive free appetizers, we charge for their drinks, and we get a lot of new business out of it. The key is to have the managers and staff really work the party hard with friendliness and good cheer to earn the repeat business.

Bottom line? Why spend $200 for a notebook of tired-out formulas from old-school marketing experts when you can open up the Yellow Pages everyday and have thousands of leads for new customers right at your fingertips?

- **Creative couponing.** Speaking of Yellow Pages, here's a great commando marketing story. In 1987 a small but popular local pizza chain in Denver was being challenged by a national chain that had just entered the market. The national chain flooded the market with full-page ads in the phone books and coupons offering two-for-one pizzas for a low price, and was really making a dent in the little guy's business. So the local pizza maker took action. They took out ads everywhere that offered the same two-for-one pizzas at the same low price. For a coupon they required you use the full page Yellow Pages ad of the new chain competitor!

"Market and advertise to each of the three 'personalities' every consumer has: the person in the workplace, the person with their friends, and the person with their family at home. People will patronize your business many times for many different reasons."

—Frank Pacetti

25

MYOB

Customer satisfaction is worthless.

CUSTOMER LOYALTY IS PRICELESS.

- **Free ice cream clobbers competitor.** In the early 1980s in Lakewood, Colorado, two mobile home companies were slugging it out for business right across the street from one another. The battle for customers was fierce with each business trying to get the customer to ignore its competitor across the road. Finally, a winner emerged with a single but deadly marketing technique that pandered to the part of human nature that can't say no to a freebie. Each customer that toured the selection of the King of the Row mobile homes was asked if they'd visited the competitor yet. If they answered no, they were each given a free half gallon of premium vanilla ice cream as a parting gift. The customer was then faced with the decision of visiting the competition across the street and letting the ice cream melt in their car or going straight home to the freezer with the free gift. Knowing human nature as you do, who do you think won? You're right.

Marketing is everybody's job. It's a philosophy, not a department. There are, of course, thousands of good cost-effective ideas to acquire new customers, and those are only a few of my favorites. I like to make my competitors work hard for their business, so while it's important to have more customers patronizing your business, I think it's just as important that they're not buying from the competition.

In the long run, remember: When the product is right, you don't have to be a great marketer. And if you've tried everything to get new business going and nothing has worked, maybe you've chosen a business that flat-out confuses the customer. Always pick a business concept that everyone understands. Why? Because as entrepreneur

Norm Brodsky says, "There is nothing more expensive than educating a market."

And, finally, don't fall into the trap of feeling satisfied with, or crowing about, how many pieces of direct mail you've sent out to your marketplace. There's a huge difference between customers coming in and customers coming back. It's more important to reach the people that count than to count the people you reach.

Customer satisfaction is worthless. Customer loyalty is priceless.

Anybody can get a customer to visit a business once. But nobody wants one-time customers. So what brings customers back with their friends? Satisfaction? Not anymore. Anyone can satisfy a customer; heck, even Gomer and Goober managed that. I want customer jubilation, not customer satisfaction.

Our performance is measured by day-to-day sales, but it's evaluated by how often our customers come in and how many friends they tell about us. Give your full focus to each customer, each experience, each transaction, one at a time. We gain customers one at a time, and guess what? That's how we lose 'em, too. Revere the "Power of One."

We all can think of businesses we've either worked in or read about whose owner's attention wavered from the customer at hand to the one he was trying to get in the front door. Or worse yet, the owner was keeping her eyes on the stock market instead of the customer. Don't lose focus on the customer you have by putting too much effort into capturing the customer you want.

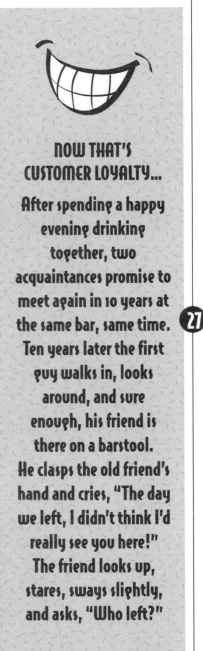

NOW THAT'S CUSTOMER LOYALTY...

After spending a happy evening drinking together, two acquaintances promise to meet again in 10 years at the same bar, same time. Ten years later the first guy walks in, looks around, and sure enough, his friend is there on a barstool. He clasps the old friend's hand and cries, "The day we left, I didn't think I'd really see you here!" The friend looks up, stares, sways slightly, and asks, "Who left?"

–Reader's Digest 7/97

SERVICE

*"**R**ight here. Right now. Tailored for me. Served up the way I like it. If the new consumer's expectations were spelled out on a billboard, that is how they would read."*
–Regis McKenna, marketing consultant

Customers patronize a business either by chance or by choice. Our objective as owners or operators is to transform chance to choice and choice to "cha-ching" by being the preferred eating, drinking, lodging, or shopping destination. Now, this is not easily said and even more difficult to do.

In the restaurant business, good food is a given but not always a must. Conversely, good service is a must but not always given. Certainly, good food is important. We know that restaurants with great menus attract great employees. But restaurants that have great menus and strong service attract not only great employees but also loyal customers. With apologies to my fellow culinarians: Good service can save a bad meal, but a great meal cannot save bad service. And who won't agree that good service makes a meal taste better? Service is our invisible product.

Service. If you want to truly understand something, try to change it.

In the history of humankind, a "market" has never bought anything. Customers buy things. And service is being radically redefined as society's power base continues to shift from those who control consumption (business) to those who consume (customers). Changing lifestyles influence consumer demands and consumer choices. As the customer changes, so changes the service need. And the customer today is experiencing more changes than Elton John at a Las Vegas benefit concert. The impact of the personal computer in people's lives has put unprecedented power, control, access, and expectations into the hands of today's consumers. Their world transforms: They can design their own software, write their own books, and get their preferred products, systems, and information customized, 24 hours a day, seven days a week. And the Internet dramatically transforms our customer's buying behaviors, service expectations—and patience tolerance levels.

Today's hospitality business owners require extraordinary flexibility and quick reflexes. In terms of products, the New Customer wants two things: wide choice and speedy access.

As Regis McKenna points out in his book *Real Time: Preparing for the Age of the Never Satisfied Customer*:

> Choice gives the customer power. An empowered customer becomes a loyal customer by virtue of being offered products or services finely calibrated to his or her needs. That amounts to a reversal of the pattern of the past, in which consumers or users of things had to rearrange their lives according to the product or service desired.

If products can be so diverse and personal, why do we still treat service as a commodity?

Executives, trainers, and HR departments traditionally have believed that service can be taught and "stored" in our employees to be doled out in equal portions to every customer. That notion is not just quaint, it's absurd. Trying to design an employee training program whose goal is "equal" service for every guest is like the farmer who tried to teach a pig to sing: It sounded horrible, and it ended up just really annoying the pig.

Service.com

"In services, acting small is big. Find ways to leverage the "build-to-order" potential of a service, to tailor it to the preferences and personality of the individual customer." –Len Berry, *The Soul of Service*

Internet search engines, like Yahoo (www.yahoo.com) and Lycos (www.lycos.com), allow you to customize how, when, and where you receive your news, mail, or information. Since 1995 Levi Strauss (www.levi.com) has been customizing jeans for its female customers. Anchor Food Products (www.anchorfoods.com) a manufacturer of frozen coated appetizers, has a web-based program called "The Anchor Customizer" that allows its restaurant customers to design and customize their own appetizer menus in cyberspace. Anchor then ships up to 150 of the newly customized menus to the restaurateur within a week. The customer can order custom point-of-sale in Jamaica or in their jammies. Or both. Anytime. 24 hours a day. All with the push of a button.

Trying to design an employee training program whose goal is "equal" service for every guest is like the farmer who tried to teach a pig to sing: It sounded horrible, and it ended up just really annoying the pig.

Can service be customized as easily as products? Certainly. When done right service is always personal, innovative, satisfying, customized. Because every transaction is separate and every customer different, service by nature has variety but must be customized to connect emotionally. "Commodity service" stinks. That's what most airlines, HMOs, health clubs–don't even get me started on health club "service"–and motor vehicle departments give us. It's almost as if they're saying, "If these damned customers would just leave me alone, I could do my job!" And, unfortunately, a variation of commodity service is creeping into the restaurant business, too. Who hasn't had dinner in one of the big chain restaurants and heard their server recite the same memorized greeting script to every other table? How does that make us feel? Special? It reminds me of the old joke: Remember, you're unique. Just like every one else.

Of course, good restaurant servers–or any good salespeople–routinely customize the service throughout the guest's visit by "reading" their customers: defining preferences through gentle questions or past experience, anticipating needs, and then suggesting food or beverage (or products or services) that might enhance the experience.

But service delivery today breaks down more often than a Barbara Walters interviewee, and the labor crunch has made it even tougher. "You have fewer people serving more customers, and the result is usually worse service," says Claes Fornell, who oversees the American Customer Satisfaction Index. So how is the hospitality industry responding? Better service, systems, and training? Some are. Many aren't. You be the judge. Quick-serve restaurants have compensated for the lack of labor by conditioning the consumer to clean his own table and tote his or her tray to

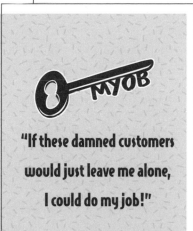

"If these damned customers would just leave me alone, I could do my job!"

the garbage can. That's more efficient for the restaurant, but I wouldn't call it better service for the customer.

One of the best things about dining in a tableside service restaurant is that it's one of the few businesses in the world where the service is mobile, it actually comes to the customer. Service used to be mobile at department stores, too. But now the standard operating procedure as a customer is to find what you want on your own and hope you don't have a question. That question will, of course, necessitate a storewide search for an associate who's facial expression is permanently set at "twenty past eight" and is either unwilling, unable, or uninterested in helping you. *So, obviously, training is an issue here, too.*

Is the System Strangling the Service?

Despite an owner's best intentions, a plethora of support systems and maze-like store design often inhibits better service, let alone allowing it to be personalized. Walk through any major supermarket or department store and experience the world of the lab rat. Go to the deli department to pick up a prepared meal to go, and then ask for some ice cream or some milk. You're immediately sent trekking 400 yards away down a frozen aisle to find your dessert, and then a further 250 yards in a different direction to the dairy cases for your lactose fix. Does a server at Denny's suggest you go to the Dairy Queen when you ask about dessert? And speaking of supermarkets...

- Why isn't there a small frozen-food case with ice cream or appetizers in the deli department? Why don't they bundle and cross-merchandise coupons

Walk through any major supermarket or department store and experience the world of the lab rat.

for flowers, appetizers, videos, wine, and desserts with every roast chicken to go?

• Why isn't there a 50-cent-off salad coupon taped to the top of every prepared meal to go at my supermarket deli?

• Why aren't there refrigerated or frozen cases closer to the floor at kids' eye level, brightly painted with dinosaurs and trains to get their attention?

• Why isn't there a smiling "Guest Service Specialist" in every supermarket deli–similar to a host or hostess in a restaurant–during busy times with a hand-held scanner? They could greet each customer with a smile and swipe their frequent shopper card. The host could be wearing a T-shirt printed with your takeout menu on it. You would be greeted by name, and–knowing what you regularly purchase from the deli based on the scanned data–the greeter could suggest your favorite (or new) items, and print out a custom coupon on the spot for a related product, like a pound of potato salad or a free movie rental. A handbasket could be offered to hold the multiple items you decided to buy. The pleasant host/hostess could then escort you to a separate cash register for easy checkout.

The answers are few, the reasons are many, but suffice it to say that most supermarkets seem designed for the customs and customer of the 1970s or '80s. As somebody once said, if you always do what you always did, you always get what you always got. The grocery industry is bemoaning its ever shrinking margins, (now on average 1.2¢ on the dollar) and fears both the restaurant business and such upstart competitors like Streamline (www.streamline.com) or Peapod (www.peapod.com) who not only sell groceries over the web, but also deliver and put them away for you, too. Now that's customization. And value. You buy both groceries and time.

Where Does a Dollar Go in a Supermarket?

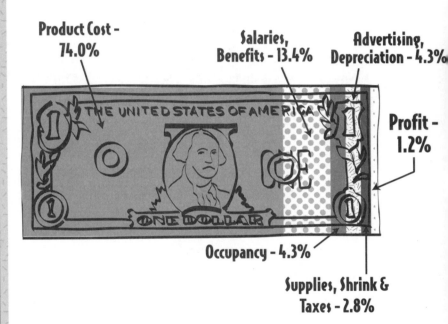

Product Cost – 74.0%

Salaries, Benefits – 13.4%

Advertising, Depreciation – 4.3%

Profit – 1.2%

Occupancy – 4.3%

Supplies, Shrink & Taxes – 2.8%

Of course, there's always another perspective to consider. *"[Product] variety, when it is broad enough, can amount to virtual customization, whether in the form of products actually sitting on the retail shelves or capable of being ordered directly from the factory in a quantity of one,"* says Regis McKenna in *Real Time*.

True, but when a business over-departmentalizes the physical layout of your product access, you proportionately

MYOB

If you're not serving the customer directly, you'd better be serving someone who is.

34

depersonalize the service experience of the customer. Not that it's stopped companies like Home Depot (www.homedepot.com) and Sam's Club (www.sams club.com) from being wildly successful. Still, always take time to evaluate and be critical of how work and service flows throughout your business and how you can improve the customer service processes affecting that flow.

Most successful businesses prioritize service over systems. "We decided not to automate our kitchens," says Outback Restaurant CEO Chris Sullivan, "because we don't want our kitchens to be system-driven. If you go too far with technology in the hospitality sector, there's a real danger that you'll forget your service should be customer-driven. You've got to take advantage of technology, but those things should be invisible to the customer."

I guess the overriding message here is that we should define service as making it easy to do business with us. How well do people enjoy doing business with you? Bill Cooney, deputy CEO of financial services giant USAA Corporation in San Antonio, Texas, challenges his employees to ask these key questions:

- Is it easy for customers to do business with us? If it isn't, why? Change it.

- Is it easy for us to do business with ourselves? If it isn't, why? Change it.

I contend that our business is our customer, not our product or service.

"Is it easy for customers to do business with us?

If it isn't, why? Change it.

Is it easy for us to do business with ourselves?

If it isn't, why? Change it."

–Bill Cooney, USAA Corporation

35

Carla Cooper, vice president of customer marketing for Coca-Cola, USA agrees, saying we need "a new breed of hospitality professional who understands that customers are the real asset, not real estate or equipment or systems."

THE THREE JOYS

Focusing on service or product instead of how to customize the experience for the customer is where most service programs fail. Actually, to be successful, service must be an enjoyable experience that should be delivered to all of the customers we identified at the beginning of this chapter: the consumer, the employee, the vendor.

Consider, for instance, the philosophy that Honda Motor Company defines as the "Three Joys:" Each person who comes in contact with the company–customer, employee, or supplier–should enjoy the experience. The hospitality industry traditionally has focused service primarily on the customer, barely on the employee, and rarely on the vendor. Maybe that's why we slice through employees like tap water through a Tiajuana tourist. There's much to be said for aligning the three partners in any business–customer, employee, vendor–in sync with our products and service delivery.

While the concept of vendors or even employees as being "partners" in our business is nothing new, perhaps the biggest "ah-ha" in this detailed examination of service in the Age of the New Consumer is that the customer must be regarded as our partner, too.

"Three Joys" Execution Strategy: Take a piece a paper and divide it into three columns. Now, put either the word customer, employee, or vendor at the top of each column. Then make a list under each column of the product and service behaviors that would make each of the trio both benefit from and also enjoy the experience of being involved with your company. For instance, a list for a restaurant employee might include recognition, energetic managers, lots of customers, health benefits, quality food, and a regular schedule. A vendor service list might detail prompt payment, friendly transactions, more business, recognition, and loyalty. Now, look at the list and decide what you need to do to provide those needs. Then prioritize the things that you can do within the next 30, 90, and 180 days. Then, do it. Just do it, dang it. If you do it, then it's done. Then next year do it better.

So we agree that to be successful in managing the heart and soul of hospitality we have to change the way we look at the marketplace. Don't just offer a product or service, offer a customized experience that connects to the consumers' hearts and minds. All customers are not created equal. So why should your service be generic? Vary service to respond to diverse customer needs.

Today's consumers are heavily experimented upon and wearily unimpressed with most of the so-called service they receive from the restaurants they patronize and the stores they shop. The good news/bad news is that the customer's demand for personalized service is high, but past experience has kept their expectations low. So it really doesn't take too much improvement to make a noticeable emotional connection service-wise with our customers. Customized customer service is a living, evolving resource that changes minute-by-minute, customer-by-customer, and interaction-by-interaction. It happens on the phone, through signage, first hand, second hand, and even back-handedly. It constantly has to be re-fed, re-focused and re-energized. And good service is not as esoteric or unmanageable as you might think.

Personalized Service: What It Is and How to Give It

What is service?

Well, what do you want it to be? To paraphrase best-selling author Ken Blanchard, the goal of effective customer service is to "satisfy" no one, but rather to create *raving fans*. A raving fan is a perennial patron, a one-person marketing campaign, a tireless booster of your company and your product. A loyalist. Maybe even a friend. Think of the people who root for teams like the Green Bay Packers, Manchester United, and the Chicago Cubs. How would you characterize their loyalty? Supporters? Or raving fans? Think of your own customers now. Supporters? Or raving fans?

Maybe the best way to create raving fans or examine best service practices is first to ask your employees and managers the question that Lee Cockerell, Executive Vice President, Operations at Walt Disney World Resort shared with me a few years back:

"What do we want to be famous for with guests?"

Your team's response will speak volumes about where you are and where you need to go. And besides, the answer to that question literally should become your company's mission statement, pure and simple.

Ask yourself: "What do we want to be famous for with guests?"

–Lee Cockerell, Executive Vice President, Operations, Walt Disney World Resort

38

Perhaps the best way of all to manage service is to follow the advice of Jan Carlzon in his groundbreaking book *Moments of Truth*. He suggests we make a detailed list of every way the customer potentially interacts with our business, our products, or our people. Then arrange them chronologically and identify which employees are integral at that "moment of truth" and what specific behavior should be demonstrated to enhance the customer's experience. Moments of truth for most businesses would include:

- Telephone calls from customers asking for directions, product information, or compliments and concerns. How well do you train your people who answer the phone to be friendly, polite, knowledgeable?

- The outside appearance of your building and parking lot. Is the physical plant and landscape clean and tidy? Are all lights working?

- The greeting they receive when they walk into your business. Energetic? Friendly? Bored?

- The cleanliness of your establishment.

- How managers appear to be enjoying their day.

- Product quality.

- How they're bid farewell and follow-up service, if any.

You get the point. There are potentially dozens of moments of truth for every department and the customer. I recommend that you conduct a detailed, moments-of-truth service audit, and make sure you get input from the service staff as well as managers. Then evaluate how to improve your employee-to-employee or department-to-department moments of truth. What gets measured gets done.

Now, you may believe that service is your invisible product, but does everyone on your team behave as if service is the savings account funding their paycheck? Well, gentle reader, a huge difference exists between belief and behavior. Allow me to illustrate by asking two simple questions:

Check one. Do you believe that health is important?
- ❏ Yes
- ❏ No

Check one. Are you currently doing things that are not particularly healthy?
- ❏ Yes
- ❏ No

That illustrates the gap between belief and behavior. Which is more important to your health: belief or behavior? Which is more important to your business? Everyone *believing* service is important, or everyone *behaving* with service-enhancing skills?

So let's focus on the specific behaviors that can customize and enhance the experience for the customer. Here's a detailed list of some of the more effective service ideas in the business. Remember, try 'em if you like 'em, and ditch 'em if you don't.

- **"From our customers."** Print those three words on every payday envelope in bold letters so your managers and staff never forget who signs their paychecks.

- **Follow the "five-foot rule."** Offer assistance to or acknowledge any customer who is standing or passing within a five-foot radius of an employee.

Follow the "five-foot rule." Offer assistance to or acknowledge any customer who is standing or passing within a five-foot radius of an employee.

40

- **The word "welcome"** should be used in all greetings.

- **Hold doors open** whenever possible for all incoming and outgoing customers. Smile!

- **Look at me/Smile at me/Talk to me/Thank me.** I first heard those four steps of service from "Coach" Don Smith in 1987, and I'm here to tell you that if you want to boil down the basic behaviors of the Four Essentials of Service, there they are. Post 'em in your employee areas in your retail store, restaurant, supermarket deli, or hotel. Those four steps are appropriate service behavior whether you're a housekeeper or hostess.

- **Make everyone a CEO.** Give every employee the power to make decisions on behalf of the customer without having to seek permission from the supervisor or manager on duty.

- **Choose your 'tude.** Cranky people annoy their teammates. Cranky people don't make customers happy. Pleasant people make customers happier. Happy customers buy more. And come back more often. You have a choice. Pick and deliver the behavior and attitude that makes dollars and sense. To paraphrase the late comedian George Burns: 'Sincerity is the most important thing in business. Once you can fake that, you can fake anything.'

- **Learn, use, and remember customers' names.** How do you get customers' names? Ask them! At our restaurants you are asked your name as soon as the hostess greets you, even if the restaurant is half full. One hundred percent of the people give their name and then ask if there's a wait. "No sir," the hostess

MYOB

THE FOUR STEPS OF SERVICE EXCELLENCE:
1. Look at me
2. Smile at me
3. Talk to me
4. Thank me

–Don Smith

"Brands are built around stories," says **Bill Dauphinais** *of Pricewaterhouse Coopers, "and stories of identity– who we are, where we come from–are the most effective stories of all."*

42

says warmly, "right this way, please, Mr. Jackson." Then she passes the guest's name on to the server and manager. The server can address the customer by name when greeting the table.

- **Grace under pressure.** A service rule: the first one to get angry loses. Sure, it's the 100th customer you talked to today, but it's the first time they've talked to you. For the restaurant or deli server, it may be "just another meal," but for the customer it's always a special occasion.

- **The answer is "absolutely!"** What was the question?

- **Share and celebrate legendary service stories** in your manuals and meetings and even advertising. Encourage your managers and front-liners to detail the "episodes of excellence" where team members went ABCD (Above and Beyond the Call of Duty) to wow a customer. Don't be outrageous. *Be real.*

- **Never greet a customer with a number.** Have you ever walked into a restaurant and been greeted by a distracted hostess who barks, "TWO?" in your general direction as she yanks a couple of menus from a rack and heads toward the dining room? You may feel she's not exactly the sharpest tool in the shed, but the antidote is quite simple: Hostess should smile and say, "Welcome! Two for lunch?" In supermarket delis greeting guests with a number is a perennial pet peeve of patrons. In front of you are shiny, clean, and beautiful display cases packed full of beautifully arranged meats, cheese, salads–and how are you greeted? "SIXTY-FOUR? NUMBER SIXTY-FOUR!"– instead of a pleasant, smiling "Good afternoon, may I help you?" Or, watch the deli clerk who is involved in another task–like wrapping cheese–and clearly annoyed that you showed up to buy something. Questions: Why is wrapping cheese more important than a customer wanting to buy a couple pounds of sliced turkey? And supermarkets should invest a few dollars training those demo people who hawk bite-sized pizza slices or Dixie cups of orange juice to be friendlier and more knowledgeable product-wise. The customer is our job, not an interruption of it.

- **Don't keep people waiting.** Customers hate to be kept waiting in person, online, or on the phone and are being conditioned, in all spheres of life, to become ever more impatient. Acknowledge new customers you can't serve promptly with a smile or a quick verbal assurance that you'll be right with them. Use eye contact to buy time–especially at the bar. Drop a cocktail napkin or coaster in front of the guest in recognition that you'll be right back. Pause for 30 seconds of silence at a training session with your service staff to give them a sense of how long 30 seconds feels to the waiting guest at a table, host stand, deli counter, or telephone.

- **Always smile when you talk on the phone.** You sound friendlier and the pleasant voice is noticed as the first Service Act in the customer's ear. Phone manners are critical for reservations, receptionists, hostesses, and room-service team members.

- **Seek out a stranger every shift.** All businesses have their regulars, whom we owners and operators naturally love. And all businesses also have their "unknowns," whom many owners overlook sometimes by paying too much attention to their regulars. In the restaurant business we say "touch every table." Make a

The customer is our job, not an interruption of it.

point of getting managers and crew to introduce themselves to the new faces every shift.

- **Watch your body language.** The way we fold our arms, our voice inflection, smiles or frowns—our body language speaks volumes to our customers. Experts have concluded that as little as 10 percent of the impact of our spoken message is carried by the actual words we use. Forty percent is carried by our "vocals" (tone, inflection, emphasis, pitch, rhythm, volume, and rate). More than 50 percent of the impact comes from body language—eyes, face, hair, gestures, posture, cosmetics, accessories, clothing, actions, and use of space. When communicating with customers or employees, it's not enough to watch what you say; you also have to watch how you say it. P.S. Don't point. It's rude. When a customer asks where the restroom or phone is, a nice alternative is for the employee to stop what he or she is doing and lead the customer halfway to the area they're looking for. Bartenders regularly violate the "no pointing" rule, usually accompanied by the warm greeting "Whatta ya need?"

- **Listening is the highest form of courtesy.** Clean off your desk when meeting with employees. Don't blurt out questions as soon as the customer or employee stops speaking, it looks as if you were formulating your reply rather than listening. Don't smile the entire time someone is talking to you; people often mistake it for mental drifting or that you're not taking them seriously.

- **Notice the color of the customer's eyes** as you introduce yourself to establish a good first

44

impression. You'll gain strong eye contact in a way that shows you're interested in what the person has to say.

- **Teach team members to pay more attention** to customers with the following game. At your next employee meeting, have someone interrupt your session by coming in with a covered tray. Under the cover are six different, even unusual, items. Display them for one minute, and then have the associate cover the tray and exit the meeting. Now, ask everyone at the meeting to write down everything they can about the person who was carrying the tray, not the items on it. The point is that too often we focus on what we're trying to sell instead of the most important detail: the customer.

- **Use hospitable conversation starters.** Making conversation with dozens of strangers hundreds of times a day is exhausting. I once was a doorman for the Fairmont hotel chain and had to be chipper and cheerful to hundreds of people for 30 seconds at a time every day. That's tough. At the end of the shift, I had to wipe off the smile with a damp cloth. But our job in this business is to make strangers feel comfortable, so here are a few topics that relax customers and ease them into our hospitality:

Compliments:

"Did you just get your hair cut? I like it!"
"You look great! Have you been losing weight?"
"That's a great tie."
"I love your earrings."
"I see you're wearing an Indianapolis Colts shirt. Are you from there?"

Children:
"Cute kids."
"How old are they? I've got two at home about the same age."

- **Recognize first-time customers.** If you could identify every first-time customer in your restaurant or deli, you'd be a winner. It costs six times as much money to acquire a new customer than to keep the one you've already got, so we'd naturally try to do everything we could to treat the new customer with a good deal of hospitality to get them to return. When you see someone in your restaurant, and you're not sure if they've visited before, don't say, "Have you ever been here before?" Because if they have you'll look, sound and feel a bit foolish. Instead, say, "You've been here before, haven't you?" That phrasing assures a positive response no matter how they answer. If they indicate this is their first visit, maybe buying them an appetizer or dessert is an appropriate how-do-you-do.

- **Control your emotions with angry customers.** Nobody likes arguing, least of all with a customer. Most confrontations can be resolved amicably if employees keep their cool, although some customers do cross the line from civility to verbal abuse. How do you keep emotions in check and customers happy? When confronted with an angry or confrontational customer, teach your employees to ask themselves a question: "Is this a problem customer, or is this person a customer who has a problem?" If you can get a grip on your emotions, you can then work on a solution.

- **Never lick your fingers at work.**

MYOB

It costs six times as much money to acquire a new customer than to keep the one you've already got.

- **Refrain from calling customers "guys."** Ladies and gentlemen are the preferred forms of address.

- **Shoot 'em and hang 'em.** Buy small plastic frames with magnetic backs with your restaurant's name and phone number on them. Take a Polaroid of your customers having fun or celebrating a special occasion at your restaurant, stick it in a frame, and give it to them to take home and put on their refrigerator.

- **Add flair to the customer's experience.** Adding flair to your service delivery and business turns customers on. Just think of how Herb Kelleher has transformed the humdrum world of airlines by adding a little flair to Southwest Airline's operations. Here are some simple ideas to try:

    Have a few pair of reading glasses handy for customers who left theirs at home. They cost around $8 each and will help guests read those great menu descriptions you've compiled.

    Teach servers and kitchen crew how to wrap leftovers in creative aluminum foil animal shapes so that customers are reminded of their dining experience the next day.

    Teach several people on your staff how to tie balloon hats. Use them for customers and children of all ages celebrating special occasions

    Don't just sing "Happy Birthday" to celebrating customers, add flair to the occasion. Sing it in Chinese. Or Hungarian. Offer to sing it backwards (turn your back and sing), the "short" version (on your knees), or the "short version, backwards under water" (holding a glass of water over your head).

Where things come from is more fun than how they're made.

48

Place Trivial Pursuit™ cards on table tops next to the salt and pepper. Unoccupied time passes slower than occupied time and anything you can do to keep customers busy and entertained adds to their experience at your restaurant. Keep a couple of newspapers at the bar for solo diners.

• **Where things come from is more fun than how they're made.** Florida orange juice. Danish ham. Texas beef. Pedigree beats process every time. Have your service team develop fun stories about your products. For instance, a restaurant server should never describe your oysters as just being "fresh." Find out their "story" from the chef and then inform the customer enthusiastically. For example tell the customer how the oysters are plucked daily, 175 miles northeast of Boston and 40 meters deep—in the coldest part of the North Atlantic—where the plumpest and most flavorful oysters grow. If you feature shishkabobs on your menu, don't stop with explaining how lamb, beef, and chicken are your featured meats. Promote the *skewers* as one of the unique features of the meal. "Yearly expeditions trek to the high plains of the ancient Burmese jungle to remove the kaba-kaba tree branches that are the source of these succulent, spicy skewers." Heck, have fun with it. Don't make your customers (and staff) suffer from the current dearth of *menu fatigue* resulting from so many same-sounding items.

And avoid the other extreme, too—those chef-as-artiste-fueled wordy descriptions of food on our restaurant menus. A fellow chef may be impressed, but to borrow a phrase from my pal, Mike DeLuca, your menu descriptions may make you sound like you don't know shiitake from shinola. For instance, read this overwrought description for spring rolls:

> *Our hummus and couscous Szchechuan cylinders are layered with line-caught organic Arctic cod and farm-raised eagle beaks marinated in a wasabi-lime-chipotle-Fruit Loops sauce, steamed in a Hopi sweat lodge, tucked in a blue corn tortilla, rolled in an enigma, wrapped in swaddling cloves, and laid in a manger of buckwheat bird's nest noodles.*

Yeah. Whatever. I'll have the burger.

- **Restaurant servers should check back within two to three bites** to make sure the meal is ideal. The quicker you discover the problem, the quicker you can provide a solution.

- **Follow up.** Call or email every customer who had a reservation or picked up a takeout order the next day to make certain their food exceeded their expectations. Also, consider a 10 percent off coupon on the next purchase or some sort of "bounce-back" coupon offer.

- **Respect the special moments of people's lives.** If you wait tables, you are a steward of very special moments in customers' lives. Restaurants are the setting for key events, like engagements, divorces, birthdays, anniversaries, first dates, weddings, reconciliations, reunions, rejuvenation, or just plain nourishment. Respect the sacred trust you have to serve, and enhance those occasions through respect, courtesy, and service. It may be just another meal to you, but to the customer, it's always a special occasion.

- **Every employee contributes to customer service.** In a restaurant the kitchen is the heart of the house. Its employees are the people who make good service in the dining room possible. To prove this point, restaurateur Nick Nickolas once gave his dishwashers the night off. Servers soon realized how important those team members are, and worked more closely with their "tableware maintenance technicians."

- **What gets inspected gets done.** A monthly customer service report is as important as a monthly P&L. How you measure it is up to you: mystery shoppers, customer letters/phone calls, or feedback forms. Either way, share the feedback with your staff publicly. If you have a kitchen staff that uses English as a second language, post service reports in the languages native to those team members. In today's high-tech world, you can even get instant feedback from diners at the same time they receive their guest check. A new wireless automated keypad from i-tech systems designed to look like a server caddy is actually a customer survey system. The customer responds to a series of brief questions that evaluate the service, meal, cleanliness, whatever you want, while they're still at the table. It can even promote upcoming events and frequent diner cards. If you haven't seen it, it's pretty cool. If you want more info, e-mail me at myob@execpc.com.

It's not just about good service anymore; it's about smart service: individual attention, customized treatment and personal pampering.

A hundred books and innumerable articles have been written about service, but I'll give you my favorite definition, and it's only six words long. Good service is "never having to ask for anything."

When Good Service Goes Bad: Resolving Complaints/Customer Feedback

"A great restaurant doesn't distinguish itself by how few mistakes it makes, but by how well they handle those mistakes." – Danny Meyer, Union Square Café, New York

In the past if a customer had a bad service experience in your store or restaurant, he or she would tell an average of 12 people about that bad experience. But in the Age of the Internet that negative experience can be told and shared hundreds of times with thousands of people for dozens of years. So it makes sense to put a premium on stopping that negative word-of-mouth before it begins with great service and customer-driven marketing. But when good service goes bad—and it will—you need strategies that will turn that frown upside down and ensure repeat business, not continuous complaints.

What you do about bad service recovery is almost as important as delivering good service in the first place. Bad Service Happens. Accept it. Look at customer complaints as a positive business experience. I believe the age old adage that for every customer who complains, there are five others who didn't and voted with their feet by going to the competition. Customers don't want their money back; they want a product that works perfectly or an experience that meets or exceeds their expectations. But most people will be forgiving—at least the first time—over a service *faux pas*.

Think positively; when customers complain, they're giving us a second chance. Use it.

One of the more effective ways to resolve a bad service incident is to understand the concept of service "plus one." That means resolving a service miscue as a priority and in a cheerful manner, and then doing one more thing on top of that literally to astound or "wow" the customer. For instance, let's say a guest orders a steak cooked medium, and it comes out rare. Standard operating procedure: the customer frets a bit, and then has to find and flag down the server. He tells the server about the problem, the server removes the plate to reheat the steak, and guess what? Everyone else at the table gets uncomfortable, unwilling to eat until their companion gets the steak back. The whole group gets edgy, nervous, wound up tighter than a cuckolded boyfriend on the Jerry Springer Show. Minutes feel like half hours.

Now, contrast that situation with a server or manager sporting the "Service Plus One" mentality. They would have checked back within two bites to discover proactively whether the guest was displeased. Next, they would politely remove the plate and offer to remove the companions' plates to keep them warm so that everyone is able to eat at the same time. Then, they would rush the re-cook, wait for it, hustle it back, stand politely nearby to make sure the steak was re-cooked to the guest's liking, and—

MYOB

Think positively; when customers complain, they're giving us a second chance. Use it.

"plus one"–buy a dessert for the guest or table for the inconvenience of having to wait for the re-cook.

Don't fight, make it right.

The most important thing to remember when you have a customer complaint is simply this: Never argue with the customer. Even if it's a questionable call, remember that the customer is not *always* right but is always the customer, and it's alright for the customer to be wrong.

The best kind of feedback is ongoing feedback, and a myriad of ways exist to get information from customers: focus groups, written or verbal evaluations, mystery shoppers, and so on. A new software program called Survey Pro even allows business owners to create all kinds of surveys that can be used via direct mail, fax, e-mail, and even through websites. It gives you the ability to create survey forms that also automatically create a database to store your data. There's even new software that allows you to customize service for repeat customers: stand-alone kiosks that can be set up in your restaurant or deli for customers voluntarily to answer questions about their experience and contribute personal information like birthdays, anniversaries, and favorite food.

And remember that the concept of "customizing" service we discussed earlier, also extends to how you collect customer feedback. If you're soliciting a "report card" from a customer, first determine how she prefers to give information to you: written, verbal, e-mail, postcard, focus group.

Summary

All companies are service companies. So, it could be argued that we're all the business of selling or marketing…promises. As Len Berry says in his book *Discovering The Soul of Service:*

> Nothing is more important to a service company's future than to instill confidence in its customers that it can and will keep its promises; the customer's confidence is a service company's most precious asset. Sustaining service is difficult because it requires sustaining customers' confidence. Labor-intensive service companies are especially vulnerable to losing customer's confidence because they must rely on people to create customer value. As these firms expand and add services, facilities, and employees, quality control becomes more problematic. As businesses become older and bigger, more complex, and more spread out, the qualities that initially made it special to both customers and employees can easily be lost. Bureaucracy replaces boldness. Turfism replaces teamwork. Formality replaces informality. Price-cutting replaces innovation. Rule-book management replaces inspired leadership.

Berry goes on to stress the importance of making emotional connections with our target markets. He challenges us to reach beyond the purely rational and purely economic level to spark feelings of closeness, affection, and trust in both our employees and customers. As Charlotte Beers, chairman emeritus of Ogilvy & Mather says: "The truth is, what makes a brand powerful is the emotional involvement of customers."

¡Chispa!

There's a great Spanish word—*chispa*—that the Seattle-area Mexican restaurant chain Azteca, owned by the Ramos family, uses to describe its style of hospitality. The word literally means "electricity," but Azteca extends the definition to mean "always being happy, staying spunky, being active and alive with every customer, creating a fiesta atmosphere and excitement" between each customer and every team member. So, do you have *chispa* running rampant in your company culture—or just service?

Getting customers to patronize us often by both chance and choice is the key to successful business. Now, how do you transform customer "visits" into profitably in this rock 'em, sock 'em business world?

Grin du Jour

A salesman rang a bell at a suburban home, and the door was opened by a nine-year-old boy puffing on a cigar. Hiding his amazement, the salesman asked the young man, "Is your mother home?" The boy took the cigar out of his mouth, flicked ashes on the carpet, and asked, "What do you think?"

—Johnathan Dingler in Quote

"It seems you can knock off anything... except awesome service."

—Tom Peters

PROFITABILITY 101

> *"If you give someone an $800,000 asset to manage, he or she will invest time at least monthly to keep that asset fresh. However, if you give that same manager the priceless asset of a human being to manage, he rarely will invest even annually to keep that asset fresh and energized."*
>
> *–Lloyd Hill,*
> *President*
> *and CEO,*
> *Applebee's International*

"❝ is a socialist idea that making profits is a vice. *I consider the real vice is making losses."*
—Winston Churchill

Condensed version of a Masters in Business Administration program: Profits can be made by producing what customers want or by making customers want what one is producing. Loss is anything that stops you from being profitable. Profit is generated by minimizing costs and maximizing sales. The end.

Cost Control

On one side of the profitability coin is cost control. On the other side is sales. Let's first look at controlling costs. "The engine that drives enterprise is not thrift but profit," said noted economist John Maynard Keynes. True. But while making money is important, it sometimes is just as important to lose less money, too.

The hospitality industry–retail, restaurants, hotels, and supermarkets–is one of the few industries I can think of where there are more ways to lose money than to make money. There's an old joke that's sad but true about the industry: How do you make a small fortune in the [restaurant/supermarket/ department store] business?

Start with a large one.

At a profit margin of less than a nickel on the dollar, controlling costs becomes a critical issue in this or any business:

I've managed a few spreadsheets in my life, but I'm no expert on the Uniform System of Accounts. In fact, I thought General Ledger was a hero of Operation Desert Storm. But I draw comfort from the realization that, like me, there are three kinds of people in the world: those who can count and those who can't.

So, let's start with the basics. Lesson number one: All money is *not* equal. For instance, $100 in sales is $100–less expenses and taxes. A $100 saved is $100. So saving money contributes to profitability. But don't get the impression that cost savings alone will win the day. I've never yet met the business owner who saved himself to prosperity. One of my favorite Dilbert comics features the pointy-haired boss plotting his profitability strategy with this conclusion: "If I cut costs more and more each week, eventually we won't have to sell anything to make money!" Saving money is good. But remember that cost control and waste watching is a process, not a meeting topic. So, we must teach our team how to think and execute "cost savings" every shift.

Here are 26 great ideas to get you going. While some of these ideas appeal directly to restaurants and hotels, each could be adapted easily for any service business:

- **Teach everyone on your team Profitability 101.** The first few pages in your training manuals or videos and one of the first topics covered live in Orientation should be the basics of gross sales versus net sales versus earnings before taxes 101. Show them how expenses relate to revenue, explain how higher costs

Teach employees how to manage their personal finances. If they're frugal at home, they'll be more frugal at work. Offer this topic in orientation for new employees and annually for current employees.

make it harder to invest money in people and training. What's the point of teaching service skills, selling skills, or cost control if there's no perspective to the Big Picture?

- **Teach employees how to manage their personal finances.** If they're frugal at home, they'll be more frugal at work. Offer this seminar annually and in orientation.

- **Post your monthly invoices** for electricity, water, heat, gas, food, beverage, insurance, and lease on bulletin boards or newsletters so that employees can relate the cost of doing business to their own expenses at home.

- **Shop your current carrier's competitors annually** for lower insurance prices.

- **Offer a 10 percent "commission"** to any employee for an idea proven to save you money. Why not? Your employees talk about areas where you're wasting money or creating unsafe conditions in your business every day. Why not ask them to share their ideas with you and then reward them for their insight with 10 percent of the money you save in cold, hard cash? Money talks, BS walks. And whatever you do, don't let those suggestions gather dust somewhere or pile up without action from you. Respond promptly to *all* suggestions and post the best for everyone to see. That helps eliminate multiple submission of the same idea and shows everybody that you take their ideas seriously.

- **Play "The Price is Right"** at employee meetings or orientation. Display everyday workplace items that employees use or abuse (in a restaurant it might include sugar packets, silverware, napkins, plates, glasses, ashtrays, table tents, menus) on a table in the front of the room with a card face down featuring the price. Employees in teams of two try to guess the right answers.

- **Reinforce "waste watching"** with posters in your work areas, prep areas, and break areas. One of my favorites is a poster with pictures of the commonly tossed, damaged, or over-offered items with their cost per unit displayed in large type. For a restaurant or deli, it might include the cost of glassware, sugar or ketchup packets, napkins, silverware, or an extra ounce of meat on a sandwich.

- **Audit your garbage.** If you run a foodservice operation, and you suspect your staff of being less than careful when they scrape dirty plates into the garbage can, here's a solution. Once a quarter, after a busy shift, distribute latex gloves to the staff and empty a garbage can at random. Go through it with the staff and see if any silverware, small plates, bowls, or glasses show up. You also may notice that a lot of your entrée side items are being thrown away, suggesting that you might want to either reduce portion size or choose a new side dish.

- **Weigh, count, inspect and verify prices on all orders.** Don't get lazy when checking in deliveries from vendors. Be routine and fastidious with each order.

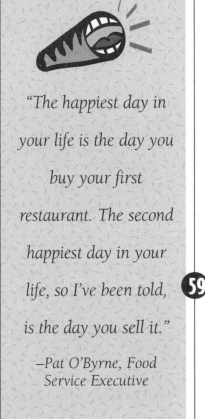

"The happiest day in your life is the day you buy your first restaurant. The second happiest day in your life, so I've been told, is the day you sell it."

–Pat O'Byrne, Food Service Executive

59

OBLIGATORY ACCOUNTANT JOKE:

Did you hear about the extroverted accountant? During the meeting he stares at your shoes instead of his own.

- **Reassess ladle size.** If you changed from a #10 to a #12 scoop for ice cream, you'd save about three cents per serving and lose less than a half ounce per portion. If you can reduce portioning slightly in prep or at the salad bar without affecting the recipe, taste, or value, consider it.

- **Display breakage publicly.** Every time an employee or customer breaks a glass or dish in your restaurant, don't just throw it away, keep it in a designated breakage bucket near the time clock that everyone can see when they clock out.

- **Raffles.** Post each employee's name every month on a sheet of paper. Choose the raffle goals based on the behavior you want to reinforce for the next 30 days: attendance, promptness, sales, working safely, cost control. For instance, if it's a cost-control raffle in a restaurant, anytime someone breaks a plate or glass, cross their names off the list. Whoever is left has their name entered into a raffle for a prize drawing.

- **Be careful stacking and washing all glasses and dishes.** Servers and bussers should avoid "glass bouquets," picking up four or five water or wine glasses at once, which causes them to chip or crack.

- **Keep knives and blades sharp.** That minimizes the cost of cuts and accidents and gives you better yield.

- **Magnetic trash-can traps** will catch most silverware before it's accidentally tossed.

- **Tag and rotate all goods**, especially perishables stored in your walk-ins or dry storage areas.

- **Follow your recipes.** High food costs in the kitchen or behind the bar can be the result of cooks or bartenders who choose to follow their own recipes or measure "by eye" instead of using the prescribed spoons, cups, scales, or jiggers.

- **Conduct random, surprise cash audits behind the bar.** In the middle of a shift, pull a cash drawer and "z" out the register. Replace with a new cash drawer. Check the register against receipts.

- **Offer a free pre-shift meal for every employee** in your restaurant or deli, if possible. That helps eliminate theft.

- **Make certain your bookkeepers take annual vacations.** A manager should take over the bookkeeping duties during the vacation.

- **Close walk-in cooler doors frequently** while loading or unloading food and beverage.

- **Keep separate financials and controls** for your merchandise and foodservice operations if you run a restaurant.

- **Talking trash?** A routine way that many restaurant employees steal is to take out the trash with something hidden in it, and then stash it behind your establishment until they leave or have a friend pick it up. Solutions? Always designate one door for arriving and exiting. Make sure lighting is bright by the back door, trash areas, and parking lot. Keep your back door secure.

"It is not the mouse who is the thief, it is the hole that allows the mouse in."

–Herman Jacobs

- **Keep it clean.** A guest or employee getting sick as a result of food-borne illness is the number one threat to your future as a successful foodservice operator. Be obsessive about your employees' safe food-handling practices and the cleanliness of your floors, counters, bathrooms, and kitchens. Train your staff to be adept at food safety and critique them daily. It is better to know it and not need it than it is to need it and not know it. Quick, what's the leading cause of food-borne-illness outbreaks? According to the International Food Safety Council, the top five contributing factors to food-borne illness in foodservice are: improper holding temperature, (59 percent); poor personal hygiene, (35 percent); inadequate cooking, (28 percent); contaminated equipment, (18 percent); unsafe food source, (11 percent). Where to get help? Contact the National Restaurant Association Educational Foundation at www.edfound.org.

- **Create a safer workplace for employees.** Besides bringing down morale, an unsafe workplace also can hurt the bottom line in terms of time lost by injured employees, repairs to equipment, interruptions in the production schedules, and overtime pay required to make up lost time. Here are two things you can do right away to make sure your workplace is as safe as it can be:

  Get better at housekeeping. Keeping floors clean, obstacles out of the way, and walkways cleared can drastically reduce the number of trips, spills, and other accidents in your workplace.

Hire a safety consultant. Have a safety consultant come in and inspect your premises–and then follow through on his or her recommendations. The typical cost for that kind of service is typically under $500, and your insurance company should be able to refer someone to you.

- **Sell more of what you have.** This may be your best cost-cutting strategy of all. And best of all, selling doesn't cost, it pays.

Watching costs obsessively is important. Period. And watching how you purchase and what you purchase is critical, too. But we don't make money buying, we make money selling.

Where Does a Dollar Go in a Restaurant?

Payroll and Benefits - 32.9%

Marketing, Promotions, Insurance - 20.6%

Profit - 4.1%

Food and Beverage - 34.2%

Rent and Utilities - 8.2%

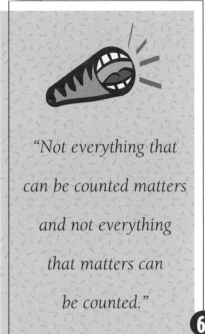

"Not everything that can be counted matters and not everything that matters can be counted."

–Albert Einstein

63

THE *Art* OF SELLING

Having a great product or a business full of customers doesn't mean you're making money. As restaurateur "Diamond" Jim Brady is alleged to have said in 1901: *"You can have the best product in the world, but if you can't sell it, you've still got it!"*

The fact is, people don't "buy" things; they are "sold" things. The best definition I've ever heard of selling is this: helping a customer make a decision that's good for them. So stop selling and start helping. Helpful selling enhances the customers' experience every time they visit your business. And if you doubt that statement, let me ask you: Who leaves a restaurant happier? The customer who spent the most or the customer who spent the least? Don't be shy about "merchandising your menu."

A long time ago, Grandpa Sullivan (a salesman so good that he could sell you a dead horse, and when you came back to complain, sell you a saddle to go with it) pointed out to me that there are only four ways to grow a business:

❶ *More customers (of the kind you want to serve)*
❷ *Improve the process*
❸ *Increase the price*
❹ *Increase the average value of the transaction*

We've already discussed creative ways to acquire more customers; we're offering ideas on improving the process in every chapter; and when you increase prices, you're asking your customers to pay for your raise or operating

---

MYOB

Who leaves a restaurant happier? The customer who spent the most or the customer who spent the least?

inefficiencies. So, that leaves increasing the average value of the transaction, which, of course, means raising incremental sales along with adding value.

Here are some strategies and tactics to improve profitability via service-driven selling:

- **A buck a customer is worth a lot.** Focus on raising your sales one dollar per person. Doesn't sound like much, does it? Not until you do the math:

  $ *Write down how many customers visit your operation in a year.*

  $ *Now, let's assume that you can increase the average spend of those customers by one dollar per transaction.*

  $ *Add a dollar sign to the left of your annual customer traffic. Example: 150,000 people per year equals a $150,000 in higher gross sales*

150,000 customers × $1 = $150,000 more a year!

And here's the beauty of raising sales a mere one dollar per person: Your fixed costs—labor, utilities, lease—don't change, so your profitability rises the more you sell. Wow! That's almost like "found" cash, isn't it? And if you run a restaurant, you know that since servers are tipped on gross, not net, sales, a dollar per person increase just added another $22,000 to the collective tip pool. I know they say that money can't buy happiness, but every server I know says, "Fork some over and watch me smile!" Would better—and more—tips positively affect your waitstaff turnover?

And maybe the best news of all relative to encouraging your team collectively to raise your sales a dollar per person is this: What costs a buck in a restaurant or deli? A soda? An iced tea? A quarter pound of roast beef? A $1.95 cup of soup shared by two people? An order of $4.95 appetizers split among five people? It's a dang do-able goal.

- **Manage profitability daily.** No matter how you currently measure sales in your restaurant, a better way is to manage sales by the square foot. It's time restaurant operators take a tip from their hospitality brethren in the retail-store arena. Have you ever done the math on how much each section or station in your restaurant generates in gross sales per year? Not many of us have, but to do so opens your eyes to some interesting opportunities in the Land of Profitability Management. Let's say you have 50 tables in your restaurant, broken down into 10 sections of five tables each. If each of those sections seat 20 customers, and you have a check average of $10 per person, that's $200 per section per turn. If you're open only at lunch and dinner, and those tables are only seated once per shift and never "turn," you still generate gross sales of $146,000 a year in that single section. That's some pretty profitable real estate! So my challenge to you is to start thinking how to better manage the profitability of each of your "mini stores:" your sections, stations, tabletops, and even window space.

For those of you with bars, you not only have retail space where the customers sit, eat, and drink, but also you have the back bar area to manage as a

Manage profitability daily. No matter how you currently measure sales in your restaurant, a better way is to manage sales by the square foot.

retail-display station. Are your brewer and alcohol vendors giving you the point-of-sale and training materials you need to help sell their products? Are they helping you maximize marketing and sales of their products in the dry storage/cold storage "real estate" that you "rent" to them? If they're not aggressively helping you find ways to use and/or sell their product more efficiently through your team, you're better off finding new vendors.

Maybe it helps to think of your restaurant sections the same way a manager of a retail mall thinks about shopping space or storefronts. Each section or station in your restaurant could therefore be considered the

server's "store"– although in our reality the restaurant operator is taking all the risk and supplies all the amenities, utilities, and products. The restaurant owner is the franchisor, the employee is the franchisee. So the savvy section manager asks him or herself these questions:

◈ *How well does each "tenant"/server maximize sales-per-square-foot?*

◈ *How well do they create flair and excitement in their "store" to induce repeat visits?*

◈ *What does the physical appearance of each of my "mini-stores" do to maximize or minimize sales?*

◈ *How can I best use the tops of my tables and wall/ceiling/floor space to display point-of-purchase merchandising displays?*

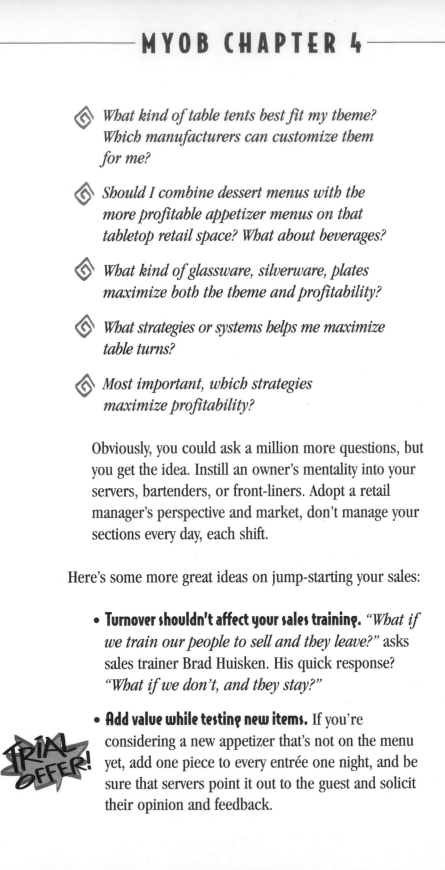

What kind of table tents best fit my theme? Which manufacturers can customize them for me?

Should I combine dessert menus with the more profitable appetizer menus on that tabletop retail space? What about beverages?

What kind of glassware, silverware, plates maximize both the theme and profitability?

What strategies or systems helps me maximize table turns?

Most important, which strategies maximize profitability?

Obviously, you could ask a million more questions, but you get the idea. Instill an owner's mentality into your servers, bartenders, or front-liners. Adopt a retail manager's perspective and market, don't manage your sections every day, each shift.

Here's some more great ideas on jump-starting your sales:

- **Turnover shouldn't affect your sales training.** *"What if we train our people to sell and they leave?"* asks sales trainer Brad Huisken. His quick response? *"What if we don't, and they stay?"*

- **Add value while testing new items.** If you're considering a new appetizer that's not on the menu yet, add one piece to every entrée one night, and be sure that servers point it out to the guest and solicit their opinion and feedback.

- **Endorse the choice.** Whenever a guest buys a product or orders a particular dish or drink, always respond, "Good choice," or "You're gonna love that." That reassures the guest and adds value to the transaction every time.

- **Shotgun selling.** This means fire at everything and something's gonna fall down. Suggest an appetizer or dessert to every customer, and the likelihood of more sales rises dramatically. I can assure you that every time you don't ask, they will say no. Every time you do ask, there's a 100 percent possibility they'll say yes.

- **Understand value versus price.** Adding value to your products or service any way you can is important, but remember that value is not lower price. As Lee Iacocca said, "People want economy. And they will pay any price to get it."

- **Appetizer menus are the portals of innovation.** The most cost-effective way to test or experiment with new menu ideas and flavors is through the appetizer menu.

- **People don't buy "products," they buy solutions.** Without getting into a lengthy discussion of Maslow's Hierarchy of Needs here, suffice it to say that customers buy things for their reasons, not yours, and those reasons are predicated on problem-solving first:

  "I'm cold. Where can I buy a sweater?"

  "I need to get to work to support my family. Where can I get a car?"

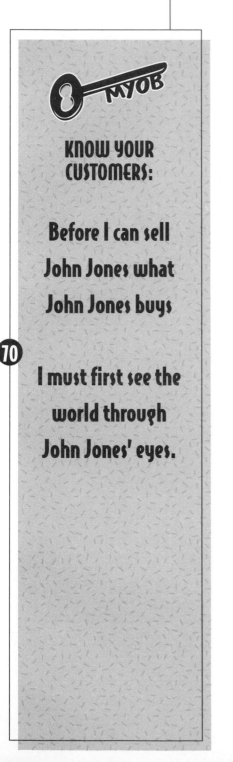

70

"I'm hungry. Where can I eat?"

"I'm bored. Where can I go to have a beer and meet people?"

"I want to try something new. What do you recommend?"

This indicates that the ability of your sales staff to read the customer is critical. It does not mean stereotype the customer; it means being friendly, establishing rapport, and asking questions to determine what they're in the mood for, and then making suggestions based on their needs, not your sales contest.

- **Restaurant servers should always subtotal guest tabs before dessert.** If the subtotal of your guest check after the entrées is $7.35, try to sell a dessert to get the tab over $10, or at least a cup of coffee to raise the tab over $8. Why? On a $7.65 tab, people will tip 15 percent to 20 percent on $7. Bumping it to $8 with a coffee sale makes the customer's thought process relative to tipping work to your advantage: You'll be tipped on $8 ($1.60) instead of $7 ($1.40) now.

- **Use colorful imagery.** Ad agencies have known for years that descriptive adjectives sell more products, and if you run a restaurant you know that the same is true for servers when they're suggesting food or beverage to your guests. Here's some words that help sell:

"Very popular"	*"One of our best sellers"*
"My favorite"	*"Fire-roasted"*
"New"	*"Good deal"*
"Family recipe"	*"Made fresh daily"*

- **Show and sell.** Menus, table tents, reader boards, dessert trays, and buttons are powerful sales tools if used properly. Why be shy about merchandising the menu in your restaurants or deli? Helpful selling means better service. My favorite sales "prop" is a button the server wears that says, "If I Don't Suggest An Appetizer It's Free."

  IF I DON'T SUGGEST AN APPETIZER IT'S FREE!

  Always "pre-market" point-of-sale items to your service staff. For instance, whenever you get new table tents in from a vendor, don't just put them on the bar or tables; post them in server stations behind the line or by the time clock so that servers see them everywhere they look. Explain, promote, and "sell" the table tents at pre-shift meetings to increase the odds of servers understanding how to use them with their guests.

- **Suggestive selling prompt cards:** If you're operating a deli, on the backside of the refrigerated display cases facing the employee always have "sales prompt" cards for each product. For instance, under Virginia baked ham, it should say, "Remember to suggest Swiss or Cheddar Cheese and coleslaw or potato salad."

- **Electronic suggestive selling prompts:** Restaurant owners should program sales prompts into their computerized point-of-sale systems so that when a server enters a dessert order, for instance, the screen automatically asks if the server suggested a specialty coffee (and specific choices are offered).

- **Pair up suggestions.** That means training your sales team to practice selling in pairs. You can do that by

Every time you want a raise, practice your suggestive selling.

playing a simple game before each shift for three minutes called "I say/You say." The manager begins: "I'm a customer, and I say 'I'll have a piece of pie, what do you say in reply, Mary?' Then, hopefully, Mary says something like: "I say, 'how about some vanilla ice cream with that?' " Or in a deli the guest says, "I'll have a roast chicken to go." You say? "Would you like to try some of our famous penne pasta salad to go with that? I'd be happy to let you try a sample."

- **Use the Sullivan "Nod."** This great piece of body language can increase incremental sales as much as 60 percent. Salespeople should smile and slowly nod their head up and down as they suggest an item to a customer. You'll be blown away by the fact that over 60 percent of the time the customer nods right back with you and takes your suggestion! For instance:

> **Customer:** "I'd like a light beer, please."
> **Server:** *"Bud Light?" (nod)*
> **Customer:** "Yeh. (nodding back) Bud Light."

The Sullivan Nod even works over the phone for room service orders (I am not making this up). It is a powerful tool. I always teach it in my seminars and videos, and I've got a file folder of no fewer than two hundred letters from salespeople and their managers testifying to its effectiveness.

- **Sample before the shift.** Try this tip from Larry Griewisch, owner of the multi-unit Jackson's Sports Grill concept in Denver, Colorado: If you want your sales team to sell more salads, entrées, appetizers, or desserts, let them try bite-sized samples before the shift. Tasting creates commitment and endorsement. Larry also recommends that your team then practices describing the items out loud to one another after they taste them so they can use the right words with their guests.

- **Free samples to waiting customers:** If you run a restaurant, and you have a 30 minute or longer wait list, have a server, bartender, hostess, or manager walk among the waiting patrons and offer free finger-food appetizers to sample (one piece per customer). Make sure the server tells the guests what they are sampling. That should be done more frequently and proactively in supermarket delis.

- **Proper layout/design boosts sales.** When designing restaurant, room service, or deli menus, don't overlook the power of placement to boost sales of your most profitable items. Consumer studies show that when perusing lists people tend to remember or focus on the first and last thing they read. That implies that we should list our most profitable items first, and our second most profitable item last on any menu. By simply drawing a box around a particular item or adding an icon next to it, "gaze motion" experts tell us that the eye is drawn to it 95 percent quicker than to other nonboxed items. These same experts suggest that eyes travel over menus in this order, and you should design accordingly.

MENU GAZE PRIORITY DIAGRAM

> *"If you're not out selling, you're being outsold."*
>
> —Bill Coban, Director, Foodservice Sales, Anchor Food Products

74

- **Promote and support sales contests.** Without a scoreboard how will the team know who's winning? I'm a big proponent of posting sales "scores" for team members. It doesn't matter how you measure it–I prefer measuring profitability rather than just gross sales–but it matters that you post it. As Ron Zemke said: "What you reinforce is what you get. What you don't reinforce is what you lose." See Chapter 5 for more contest ideas.

- **Think "capture rate."** When measuring employee contests, remember that statistics are like bikinis: What they reveal is interesting, but what they conceal is vital. In a recent issue of *Promotions* newsletter, Brian Williams from the Doubletree Hotels offered this advice: "If you only look at straight [volume] numbers, then your busy shifts will always produce the 'winners.'" Instead, Brian suggests focusing in on the upselling "capture rate." He explains: "If a server sells three out of 10 people a featured product, then the capture rate is 30 percent. You want to reward the employee who is most successful with these numbers."

- **Have servers compete with their own sales "records."** *"Selling competitions succeed when a server competes with his or her own track record,"* says Jay Cone, former director of human resources for East Side Mario's in Dallas. Jay gives this example: If your records show that a particular server usually sells one appetizer for every seven entrées, challenge her to increase the ratio to one in every five. At East Side Mario's, the company splits the additional profit with the server 50-50.

If you sell something you believe in to someone who really does want or need what you have, it's a win-win situation, a beautiful thing. Summary? Simple:

If you're not out selling, you're being outsold.

BONUS SELLING TIPS FROM THE TRENCHES

Suggest appetizers before you take the first beverage order.

Always say "Be sure to save room for dessert" when seating guests or delivering their entrées.

When recommending a favorite menu item to a customer say "If you don't like it, we'll buy it. No risk."

Hostesses should suggest a specific appetizer, dessert or beverage to every guest they seat.

Pre-sell to customers who make reservations over the phone. "Since this is a birthday party, should we chill a bottle of champagne for you?"

Point out other guests enjoying the item you're suggesting. "The Reese's Peanut Butter Pie is delicious. It looks just like what that table is sharing."

Jim Sullivan's
TOP 10 SIGNS
A BAD RE

10 You ask for change for a dollar, and the waitress asks if you have anything smaller.

THEY'VE GOT POISON CONTROL ON SPEED DIAL. **9**

8 THEY'RE OPEN 24 HOURS, BUT THERE AREN'T ANY GARBAGE CANS OUT BACK.

The manager's name is Heimlich. **7**

6 The Waitress uses apron stains to point out the daily specials.

pea soup

blueberry pie

76

YOU'VE GONE TO ... BAD RESTAURANT

You suddenly realize it's the <u>water</u> **5** that's amber colored, not the glass.

4 AFTER PRESENTING THE FOOD, THE WAITER SAYS, "GOOD LUCK!"

 They've got PEPTO BISMOL on draft. **3**

2 YOUR burrito turns out to be a rolled-up Ace bandage.

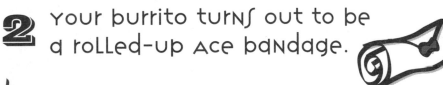 ...and the #1 sign you've gone to a bad restaurant?

 *The only thing "French" about the chef is the way he's <u>kissing your wife!</u>* **1**

TEAM

> ## "Be loose and have fun."
>
> **–The first sentence in the Great Harvest Bread Company's mission statement**

"*Create an environment of care for your employees and they in turn will care more about your customers, profitability and growth of the business*"
—Lloyd M. Wirshba, American Express Company

Who's more important to our business success: customers or employees? Ten years ago 90 percent of us probably would have replied: "customers." Now, the answer is not so clear cut. I think the question is irrelevant to the Big Picture of building loyal customers, happy employees, and profitable operations. It's a "chicken and egg" proposition; who came first in a successful business– repeat customers or outstanding team members? They're both important and your business will fail without an adequate supply of either. So this chapter will focus on three key issues relative to building a Kick Butt Team:

❶ How to find, hire, and retain the best employees.

❷ How to develop them into appreciating assets through daily education and training.

❸ How to recognize, renew, and reward your employees and managers.

In today's business world, if a company is turning over too many employees, it is losing value simultaneously. The two biggest challenges any business owner faces in the new century is retaining the best people and improving their

productivity. This following chapter is chockablock full of creative new hiring, training, and employee contest ideas to help you keep your best people and make your best better…and brighter.

Job of the past…or the future?

"We are looking for a self starter, motivated, dedicated, experienced manager who will accept full responsibility without the authority. Must be willing to work 70 to 80 hours a week, including 40 hours of shift work. We offer no training, low pay, no benefits, no incentives, and no vacation. Ideal candidate would be able to squeeze as much money as possible out of a property with 150 percent turnover, no vacation or benefits for the employees, and very little working capital. If you meet these qualifications, are not sensitive to constant criticism, or susceptible to burnout, we want you on our team."

Sound familiar? Not too long ago, that unofficial job description was accurate for most restaurant, hotel, supermarket, or retail managers. And unfortunately, in many cases, it still is. Who's to blame for the bad rep that the hospitality industry has as a career choice? The press? Politicians who characterize dead-end careers as "burger-flippers?" No.

We are to blame. Our traditional pattern of low pay, no benefits, and long hours have made our workplace reputation weaker than a mixed drink in a strip club. Arnold Donald, chairman of the Monsanto Company, says, "Have three people do five jobs but pay them like four."

MYOB

We don't have a labor crisis. It's a turnover crisis.

Great advice. Unfortunately, many hospitality operators have used a different formula: Have three people do four jobs but pay them like two. As one disenchanted waitress recently told me: "People do what you pay them to do, not what you ask them to do." Ouch.

Most of our best and brightest don't even consider the hospitality industry to be a "real" job. Because of the perception of the way we've treated young workers the last 10 to 20 years, we've created a generation of potential "image terrorists" who will probably end up bad mouthing our industry for the next 40 to 50 years of their working life to anyone who'll listen. Double ouch.

So what's a hospitality professional to do? While most big restaurant, hotel, supermarket, and department store chains have begun to take better care of their internal customers, there's still a collective need industry wide to make our employees' work lives more meaningful, better compensated, and less stressful. If we can accomplish that, maybe we can admit that we don't have a labor crisis. It's a turnover crisis. Who won't agree that employee turnover has an impact on customer service and repeat business? Customers like to see the same employees every time they visit. They like to be recognized. It's not only comforting, it's a competitive advantage. The competition for workers in our industry is inspired by competition for customers. There is an absolute link between happy workers and happy customers.

Where to begin? Everybody in the hospitality arena seems to be fishing for the same employee from an ever-shrinking labor pool. "Corporate America hires people for what they know and fires them for who they are. Hire people who fit your culture, and then train them in the business," says

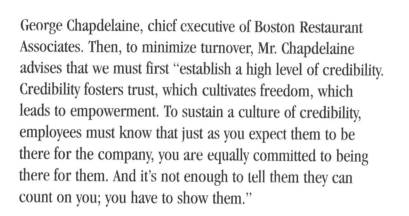

George Chapdelaine, chief executive of Boston Restaurant Associates. Then, to minimize turnover, Mr. Chapdelaine advises that we must first "establish a high level of credibility. Credibility fosters trust, which cultivates freedom, which leads to empowerment. To sustain a culture of credibility, employees must know that just as you expect them to be there for the company, you are equally committed to being there for them. And it's not enough to tell them they can count on you; you have to show them."

Cash is not King, but "Meaningful" is Money

Employees today will not be wooed, motivated, or retained by money alone. More and more workers choose their employers based on a criteria of "meaningfulness"–social responsibility, work/family balance–where personal and professional growth couple with learning as a vital part of the job.

Employees want more attention paid to their work schedules, more flexibility, more accommodation to their lives outside of work. Quality of life–including quality of life while on the job–matters more to today's workforce than ever before.

So it stands to reason that when a manager helps employees balance their work lives with the rest of their lives, they feel a stronger commitment to the organization. The current emotional angst presiding in the workplace is a loss of personal equilibrium. What makes people feel out of balance is that they have a certain set of values, what they believe in, and what they feel is important, and then it doesn't match what they have and what they do.

In a business where good employees are harder to find than a dishwasher on a 10-minute smoke break, managers, owners, and operators must re-think their priorities. Many experts contend that the customer doesn't come first anymore; the employee does. Do you agree or disagree? Here's a hypothetical situation to test your perspective no matter what kind of business you operate:

> *You have a customer who eats in your restaurant once a week, 52 times a year. You also have the world's best hostess/greeter. She gets to work on time, always smiles, remembers guests by name, and consistently suggests appetizers and desserts to every guest. Imagine that tomorrow one of them has to go. Who do you vote to save?*

There is no right answer. I'd hate to lose any customer, but an employee who is positively influencing that many people each shift is a keeper. That's a good exercise to share with your managers and team mates to test employee-guest value.

Do You See What I See?

To help align your thinking visually with the new realities of the marketplace, let's diagram the typical organizational hierarchy of most businesses:

OWNER/OPERATOR

MANAGERS

FRONT-LINE SUPPORT

FRONT-LINERS

CUSTOMERS

Look that pyramid over carefully. This top-down power perspective is medieval in design and overly paternalistic in execution. Who's the most important person relative to a profitable business? The customer. So why are customers on the bottom of the pile? Let's flip that pyramid upside down and see our business from a different perspective:

CUSTOMER
FRONT-LINERS
FRONT-LINE SUPPORT
MANAGERS
OWNER/OPERATOR

Now, that is hardly a new management idea, but one we should revisit frequently, lest we lose our "place." This perspective puts the hierarchal order in a truer light: the customer and front-liner on top, meaning quite simply that we need to be responsible to the customer and the employee, not the boss. Who is the only person in your company present at the point-of-purchase? It's not the owner, it's the front-liner—the server, bartender, deli server, salesperson. Who's right behind them? The support staff—bookkeepers, kitchen crew, stockers. We as managers and operators are rewarded not for what we do but for what our employees do. If you're a manager, you're hired by the people you report to but fired by the people who report to you. Their performance is your paycheck. Their lack of performance is your butt. In a manner of speaking, of course.

Way back in chapter two we suggested that the "function of our business is to acquire and maintain customers." That same objective applies to our internal customers—our employees and managers as well. So let's outline some creative sourcing and hiring ideas.

Finding Keepers: How to Source and Hire Good Employees:
"While looking for a job, never answer a telephone early in the morning by saying, 'This better be good.' "–Richard Moran, *Beware of Those Who Ask for Feedback*

To hire effectively and stop employee turnover, a successful business focuses on sourcing for talent; creative interviews; dynamic orientation; employee development/ nurturing and effective recognition; incentives; and rewards.

Sourcing for Talent

One restaurant manager I know in Upper Montclair, New Jersey shared his hiring strategy: "We have two basic criteria for filling positions–They must be alive and from this planet." Minimal standards, to be sure. But it's a fact that slim pickings characterize the labor pool these days. And it may not get better in the near future. There are 44 million 18- to 31-year-olds versus 78 million baby boomers. That means that not only are there fewer 18- to 31-year-olds, but also fewer good ones. According to the National Restaurant Association, demand for foodservice managers is expected to grow by 35 percent in the next six years, the highest of any restaurant occupation. So, if you think the battle for workers and managers is tough now, look up "competition" in the dictionary and you'll find (and will continue to find) a picture of the hospitality industry.

So where do we begin? Do we hire the experience or the personality? The warm body or the budding talent? Peter Carbonara shares this perspective in *Fast Company* magazine: "What separates [a company's] winners from their losers, good hires from bad? The answer is what people know is less important than who they are. Hiring is not about finding people with the right experience; it's about finding people with the right mind-set. Hire for attitude and train for skill."

Hire Power

Get hip. Don't use methodologies developed in the 1970s and 1980s to deal with the realities and scarcities of the labor pool in the 21st century. Forget newspaper ads if you're looking for good hospitality employees. Those are the last places they look for a job. Here are some creative sourcing ideas from a variety of successful restaurants, hotels, and supermarkets:

- **Think like a marketer.** That is probably the best way to start sourcing new employees. Talk to the people who have already "bought" your product–your current employees. Find out what attracted them to your business and why they stay. Write down the key words they use. Ask them to help design ads or marketing programs to help attract new employees to your operation.

- **Make jobs easy to apply for and hard to get.** Allow 24/7 access to job application at your business. Gone are the days when we could say "applications accepted between 2 PM and 4 PM" or even "10 AM to 5 PM." Your best employee probably is working somewhere else right now. Allow them to apply when they have the time, not when it's convenient to you. Many hospitality companies have Internet-based or 1-800 pre-screening application processes. It's a new millennium. What's your hold up?

- **Realtors.** Befriend real-estate agents that patronize your business. They obviously have an inside track on who's moving into the area. Maybe the transplants are looking for work in a restaurant, deli, or retail store. Maybe one of the spouses are former managers who could help you fill a position.

- **Movie theater previews.** We've all seen ads for businesses on slides shown before previews in movie theaters. Why not put an ad there advertising the job opportunities at your place? Some 70 percent of Americans aged 18 to 34 go to the movies on the weekends. Isn't that your target audience?

- **Restaurant employee favorite bars.** If you're looking for restaurant employees, one of the more creative ways to find them is to talk to the bartenders at the watering holes hospitality employees frequent.

- **Silver handcuffs.** This term refers to the practice of "longevity bonuses," or holding a certain amount of bonus money aside each year for managers that is payable only in three-year increments.

- **Bounties for referrals.** Any employee who refers a new associate gets a $50 cash bonus after the new employee is hired and satisfactorily completes 90 days.

- **Wage guarantees.** Wherever you recruit in print, promise to meet or beat the prospective employee's current wage (paycheck stubs as proof is required).

- **International students.** Many restaurants, resorts, and hotels, especially on the East Coast, recruit and hire European students for their seasonal peaks.

- **Be where the employees are.** "High-tech" and information companies routinely recruit on ski slopes and beaches during school breaks. High

"…*what people know is less important than who they are. Hiring is not about finding people with the right experience; it's about finding people with the right mind-set. Hire for attitude and train for skill.*"

–Peter Carbonara, in *Fast Company* Magazine

school job fairs and Junior Achievement programs are great places to talk about your company and find part-time employees.

- **Source the people you already know.** In conversations with customers, suppliers, vendors, local hotel/restaurant school alumni, or current employees, always ask if they know anyone who would be interested in joining your team. After all, you're never "fully" staffed.

- **Carry your business cards everywhere you go.** If you experience great service at a car wash, CD store, or dry cleaners, offer the employee who exceeded your expectations your business card and let 'em know you're interested if they're ever looking for part-time work.

Hiring the right person saves you a ton of time and effort later on. After all, it's easier to hire nice than it is to teach nice. "The standard hiring process–a resumé, interviews, some references–may tell you about history and hypotheticals," says CEO Cliff Oxford of Atlanta-based Support Technologies. "But it says little about how a candidate can add value to your company today. You end up taking a leap of faith. You can't do that anymore."

Creative Interviews

"A resumé is a balance sheet without any liabilities."
–Consultant Robert Half

Let's assume you used the creative employee sourcing techniques detailed above, and now you have an available pool of potential team members from which to interview.

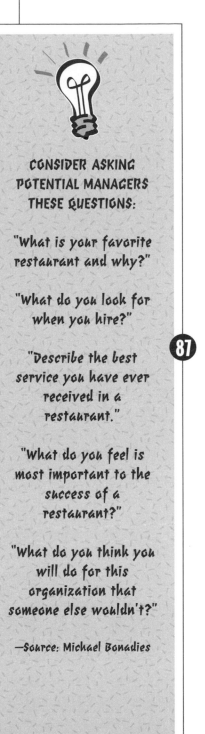

CONSIDER ASKING POTENTIAL MANAGERS THESE QUESTIONS:

"What is your favorite restaurant and why?"

"What do you look for when you hire?"

"Describe the best service you have ever received in a restaurant."

"What do you feel is most important to the success of a restaurant?"

"What do you think you will do for this organization that someone else wouldn't?"

—Source: Michael Bonadies

The concept of how to conduct effective interviews could fill a book; indeed, there are dozens on the topic at your local bookstore. So I'm going to limit my discussion to brief, key points, like:

- Follow all applicable federal, state, and local laws.

- Ask the questions you're required to ask by your organization.

Consider asking these questions as well:

 "Tell me about the best manager you've worked for. Why was he or she a good manager? What would your ideal boss be like?"

 "What was your least favorite manager like? How did you handle the things you didn't like about him?"

 "Tell me about a disagreement you and a previous boss had. How did you resolve it?"

 "Tell me about your first job." You'll usually get a more enthusiastic response than discussing their last job.

 Mike Hurst, owner of the 15th Street Fisheries restaurant in Ft. Lauderdale, Florida suggests asking this question to get a sense of the potential employee's personality: "What's the funniest thing that ever happened to you?"

 "If I were your boss, what would be the most important thing for me to say or do to support you?" (from *Getting Commitment at Work* by Michael C. Thomas)

The best person you interview isn't necessarily the best person for the job.

88

And, finally, after the candidate answers all of the "official" questions, ask yourself these questions to determine your "gut feel" for the person's natural friendliness and competitive value:

"How would I feel if this person was working for the competition?"

"Is this someone our teammates would want to go out and socialize with?"

When you do find the right person for the job you have, try to hold off telling the other candidates that they weren't chosen–at least until the new employee starts. You can be left stranded if prospective team members change their minds at the last minute or accept another offer. If you quickly tell the other qualified candidates that you've chosen someone else, you'll probably lose them. *But don't string candidates along.* It's wrong to wait until you're satisfied with the new employee; wait only until you're sure the prospective employee or manager actually is coming to work for you.

Dynamic Orientation

You never get a second chance to make a good first impression. The first day on the job is filled with high expectations and anticipation. After all, the ads said "fun, exciting, team atmosphere." But how many of us have felt betrayed or short-changed on the first day of work? You get the job and an enthusiastic welcome at the interview. Then, on Day One you're greeted by a surprised manager who wasn't aware of your start date, calls you Tim instead of Jim, hands you incomplete or disorganized training materials, and pushes you off to an unprepared team member to "show you around." As L.L. Bean once said: "Make sure that the story isn't better than the store."

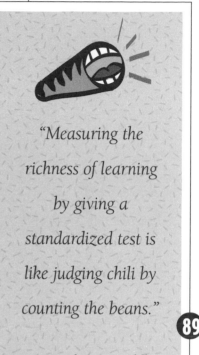

"Measuring the richness of learning by giving a standardized test is like judging chili by counting the beans."

– Daniel Feri, Middle School Teacher, Lombard, IL

89

"I like to ask a potential management hire if they consider themselves a teacher. If they say 'yes', I ask them to give me 3 examples. If they say 'no', I probably won't hire them. Great teachers make some of the greatest leaders."

–Lee Cockerell,
Executive Vice-President,
Operations
Walt Disney World Resort

Here are some suggestions for a dynamic welcome and effective orientation:

- **Be prepared.** Extend a formal and friendly welcome to the new team member in the mail with a hat or t-shirt

- **Hand them a comprehensive Employee Kit**, including training materials, a floor plan, name spelled out in calligraphy on the cover, and name badge.

- **Many employee-friendly businesses** post a new team member's biography by the time clock that includes favorite music, movies, TV shows, books, and a Polaroid photo. Those bios and pictures could be done for every new and current employee and manager, and then assembled into an employee "Yearbook."

- **The general manager should conduct an official store or restaurant tour.**

- **Assign a specific "buddy" or team mate** to be the "go-to" person for questions or guidance when a manager is not available. It should be someone other than a manager.

- **Managers should conduct informal New Employee Orientation Meetings (NEOM)** after the first 30 days to debrief the new associates and answer or clarify any questions, criticisms, or concerns.

- **A detailed Development Schedule Plan (DSP) and Development Tracking Sheet (DTS)** should be presented and discussed. Those forms should detail every task and expectation associated with the position and have places where the new employee, the trainer, and the manager can initial that they both understand

and can perform the task described. Have the new team member begin by self-assessing his or her skill level by checking off a "Can Do" or "Can't Do" box for each task. That will both build their confidence and clarify their expectations.

Development and Nurturing

"There are two reasons why people leave their jobs. Either they don't feel appreciated or they don't like their boss." –Andy Pearson, CEO, Tricon Global Restaurants

First things first: Of all the people who will never leave you, you're the only one. OK?

Now that that's out of the way, two questions: Is a "Help Wanted" sign the only thing that's permanent about your labor force? And if your retention rate were a movie, would it be titled *Hire Today Gone Tomorrow*?

Everyone who works for you is a volunteer. If you work in the foodservice industry, you can get on the phone and have a new job in five minutes. How's that for pressure? Even employees who start out strong, motivated, and enthusiastic can lose their verve after a few months. "Beware of the 91st day flu," says Ken Wasco, of Gordon Food Service in Grand Rapids, Michigan, "meaning employees who do well for the first 90 days, then the veneer cracks on the 91st. Your first clue that they're becoming disenchanted with the job? When you cheerfully ask them how they're doing, and they glumly reply, 'I'm here.'"

First things first: Of all the people who will never leave you, you're the only one. OK?

91

Of course, some turnover is good. But where do your start to control or eliminate involuntary employee *churnover*? Impress on your people by deed and example that you're good, smart, worthy of their loyalty and "followership." Make them want to be part of the good fight. Demonstrate that you will be an advocate for your team as well as the customer. And don't let tired myths about customer service replace respect or inhibit sharing information. Here's a classic one to debunk with your team ASAP: "The customer is always right."

The customer is not always right.

Employees know when customers are wrong. The "all-knowing" customer is, in fact, one of the biggest turnoffs for the otherwise motivated employee. If we insist that the customer is always right, then in every dispute the employee must always be wrong. And that ain't right!

(The Customer is Not Always Right)

As one reader wrote in a letter to *Fast Company* in 1998: "Besides, who cares who's right or wrong? We're in business to fix problems, not to fix blame. Our job is to help customers be successful, not to pretend they're infallible. Why not encourage employees to see themselves as detectives, coaches, and partners/advocates for the customer, even when the customer is wrong? Please don't encourage employees to endorse a motto they don't find satisfying—and that doesn't represent reality. Instead, find

better ways to capture the nature of your relationships with customers. They'll be happier, and so will you."
The customer is not always right, but is always the customer, and it's alright for the customer to be wrong.

Improve compensation.

This is such a sensitive topic in the hospitality industry today. We howl and wail about our image as burger-flippers and a dead-end career, but the truth is, we've underpaid and underbenefitted our teams for years. Granted, an average profit of four cents on the dollar does not inspire paycheck philanthropy, but we've gotta step up to the plate with a host of new pay packages and creative incentives. The rest of this chapter will detail some of the more effective ideas for incentives and rewards. Barry Mehrman, staff and employment development director for McDonald's, calls competitive wages "the greens fees," meaning the price of playing the employment game. Beyond that, he says, "other benefits become the competitive advantage." Layer on the incentives—401 (k) plans, health insurance, bonuses. There also must be a balanced and equitable distribution of performance-based incentives and rewards. It's actually a smart time-saving device in a way. In this era in which a typical restaurant chain will go through 25 resumés to get one good manager, remember that it's cheaper and easier to give employees a raise than trying to replace them.

In order to make magic in the workplace, inspire purpose and passion in our people, and reduce churn in our workforce, we must add "flair" to the employee's experience every shift. It starts with a commitment from managers to be cheerleaders, overly enthusiastic, silly, crazy, nuts in the ways they create, channel, and challenge the energy of the crew and the work environment each and every shift. Remember: Your employees would rather work for the inspired leader lighting the way with a blowtorch than a manager holding a candle. My challenge to managers? Every day, when you come to work, the score is zero. What's it gonna take to hit it out of the park today? Here are a couple of ideas on how to pump up the volume.

Add Flair to the Employee's Experience:

- ⊚ **Create a feeling of membership, not employment.**

- ⊚ **Implement quarterly employee satisfaction surveys** to clue you in if employees are getting back what they expected when they joined your team.

- ⊚ **War stories inspire loyalty, train teammates, and create commitment.** Collect your best stories from your team about great service, inspired commitment, people who went above and beyond the call of duty, etc. Feature those "legendary service" stories in your meetings, training manuals, and company culture. A good question to ask your teammates to get the process started is this one: *Do you have a story about working here that you wish everyone knew?*

- ⊚ **Give small, unexpected rewards for jobs well done.** When you see a team member go out of her way to give extraordinary service or to help another associate out, or a cook who handled an unexpected lunch rush perfectly, hand them a quick-pick Lotto ticket, a candy bar, a thank-you note, a scratch-off lottery ticket. Show appreciation for a job well done while it's top of mind and fresh in memory. Praise is

---

THIS JOB IS A TEST. IT IS ONLY A TEST. HAD IT BEEN AN ACTUAL JOB YOU WOULD HAVE RECEIVED RAISES, PROMOTIONS, RECOGNITION, PRAISE, ENCOURAGEMENT, AND DAILY TRAINING.

—GRAFFITI IN EMPLOYEE BATHROOM AT AN ITALIAN RESTAURANT CHAIN, DALLAS, TX

94

like champagne–it should be served while it is still bubbling. At employee meetings always recognize these "little victories" aloud so that other team members can both recognize and learn from the service or sales-driven behavior.

◎ **Assign one person or team of two to be in charge of the employee bulletin board each month.** That will give you a fresh look, fun style, and creative competition. Most important, it may result in the information on the bulletin board actually getting read.

◎ **Ask employees to complete an essay that begins: "If I ran the company..."**

◎ **Have each team member identify MODD** (What Makes Our Day Difficult) in writing and then initiate a process to eliminate those difficulties. Or post this question with a blank sheet on your employee bulletin board: "What made you mad today?" Make sure you follow up on solutions.

◎ **Put the words "Suggestion Box" on the general manager or store manager's office door.**

◎ **Consider instigating a company "concierge" service** to help employees with personal details they may have forgotten (i.e. flowers to spouse on anniversary, birthday card to Mom, etc.) Sound corny? Starbucks has been doing it with great success for the last several years, and their employees love the value-added benefit.

◎ **Let team members determine the weekly schedule.** For instance, one successful restaurant I know of assigns two servers to each shift and lets them

Put the words "Suggestion Box" on the General Manager or store manager's office door.

95

decide who works when. Teammates will be more willing to cover for their partners when they know the favor will be returned.

- **Let your team serve each other.** If your organization has a sick day policy, allow team members to give each other unused sick days when unexpected illnesses or injuries occur.

- **Raise the bar.** Eliminate "average" ratings from your employee appraisal forms. You'll spur your teammates to try harder for above average ratings.

Tips for Making Meetings Memorable

Humorist Dave Barry has good advice for managers who have employees who fall asleep in meetings: *"Have everybody leave the room, then collect a group of total strangers, from right off the street, and have them sit around the sleeping person and stare at him until he wakes up. Then, have one of them say to him in a very somber voice, 'Bob, your plan is very risky, but you've given us no choice but to try it. I only hope, for your sake, that you know what the hell you're getting yourself into.' Then, they should file quietly from the room."*

Effective communication is your secret weapon in the battle against complacency, turnover, and indifferent customer service. And effective communication revolves around meeting in groups of one or more. So, how do you get the most bang out of your meeting buck? Well, first, we ante up a few truths about the subject. Ask most employees if they like meetings, and the majority will respond that they'd rather build a pig from a kit. Most employees dislike meetings. And with good reason. The majority of them are poorly organized, routinely

"One of my favorite words is 'miscommunication'. Its meaning has become so broad as to justify everything from the Middle East crisis as to why a relative missed the wedding. In the business world, vendors and clients alike use it to explain away huge mistakes, and, best of all, without assigning responsibility to anyone. It's the verbal Get-Out-of-Jail card for the New Millennium."

–Joe McDonald

unfocused, and often cornier than Kansas in August. But meetings are critical for imparting knowledge, delivering training, sharing information, and improving performance. So here are some simple suggestions for staging and executing successful and engaging employee meetings:

- **Hold meetings routinely, not just in crisis.** At least one all-employee meeting every quarter, a mandatory three minute, pre-shift meeting in each department every day.

- **Use meetings to celebrate, communicate, praise, and problem solve.**

- **Make them fun.**

- **Involve everyone**—either through planning or participation.

- **Rehearse, videotape and critique all presentations.**

- **Write down an agenda and expected outcomes of the meeting.**

- **If you have many topics to cover in your meeting**, address the easiest to cover items first and save the more complicated ones for later in the meeting. By blowing through a series of topics quickly early, on you send the message that the meeting is about accomplishing things. Starting with the more complicated topics can bog down the entire meeting.

- **Begin and end all meetings on time.**

- **Invite top performers to speak** and share their techniques and advice. Since they're part of the team, they'll have instant credibility and relevance.

Self-confident employees serve better and sell more. And if you want to improve self confidence, you do it by training.

- **Avoid "all-lecture" format.** Help employees find team solutions to pressing service, sales, or cost-control challenges by working in small groups to "discover" information. Compliance with the solutions they provide should be a no-brainer since people never argue with their own data.

- **Talk about the employee's feelings and needs first.**

- **Talk about the company's or your feelings and needs second.**

- **Write down all ideas without evaluating.**

- **Set a timetable for solutions or idea implementation.**

Kindness and consideration shown is like pennies invested for dollars returned. Managers who routinely use the so-called "soft skills" to jazz up their staff and brighten the workplace will go a long way to minimize turnover, maximize retention, and energize profitability. Maybe the best idea to create value in your team's experience is to teach them something new everyday. But stop training–start *learning*.

Knowledge Management 101: Or Why TRAINING DOESN'T WORK...And What We'd Better Do About It
"To teach is to touch the future."
–Ted Fowler, CEO, Golden Corral Corp.

People, in general, enjoy learning, but they hate being "trained." Animals are "trained." People prefer development. Most employees in the hospitality arena resist or resent training because of past experience either in the public school machine or at the hands of a boring

instructor who was to inspired learning what Pauly Shore is to acting. Plus most, if not all, hospitality employees believe that they already have the requisite skills to do their job reasonably well. But then we schedule them for "training" and immediately the resentment barriers are raised and before you know it…well, as restaurateur Mike Amos says, "the ears have walls." Don't blame the employee for dissing training. As Aristotle so aptly put it: "If the son swears, strike the father."

Most company training programs feature way too much teaching-by-telling and way too little learning-by-doing. Example? You didn't learn to ride a bike in a seminar, did you? In fact, the whole premise that you can "train" a new recruit to act just like an "ideal" someone else is outdated and unrealistic. And the ugly truth is that training is viewed as a joke in many companies today. Most employee manuals and training sessions reflect workplace reality as accurately as the Roadrunner cartoons portray the Laws of Physics. If your trainers rely on lecture, videos, manuals, memorization, and tests, you're in deep caca. *Deep* caca. You can't just talk or "test" an unknowledgeable worker out of ignorance. If we as an industry do not find a better way to teach people how to do their jobs, we're headed for serious trouble.

YOU TOO, CAN RIDE A BIKE – 12 EASY STEPS!

It's time for everybody in your company to pay more attention to training and the impact it has on your people, performance, and productivity. Helping team members attain key skills and concepts quickly and confidently is a key competitive advantage, not just a "training tool." If you direct your company's fortunes from the owner or CEO's seat, you'd better start caring about how your people learn and how your trainers are helping them acquire knowledge and skills. The fact is that training isn't just for trainers anymore.

Prescription before diagnosis is malpractice, so let's begin by asking a simple question: What's wrong with much of today's training? Roger Schank, in his book, *Virtual Learning* , sums it up succinctly:

> Everything that's wrong with training can be summed up in four words: It's just like school. School isn't really about learning; it's about short-term memorization of meaningless information that never comes up later in life. The school model was never intended to help people acquire practical skills. That fact, however, hasn't deterred business from adapting this model. Memorize the teacher's words; memorize the training book's policies and procedures.

What department in your company will experience the greatest change in the next decade? Training. What department in your company will have the greatest impact relative to employee retention, skills, energy, resolve, service, and sales? Training. What department in your company will CEOs, owners, and operators focus on the least, attention-wise? Training.

Your Secret Weapon

Look, maybe you think I sound like a manure salesman with a mouth full of samples, but I'm here to tell you that training is the Hydrogen bomb of competitive business weapons. And it's evolving quicker than a genetic sheep in a Scottish biology lab. There is nothing short of a

Use "I messages" when discussing performance issues with team members: "I feel (name a feeling) about (name a behavior) because (state your reason)."

That effective technique works for both problems and praise at big meetings or in one-on-one discussions.

revolution in learning going on in the workplace today. A fascinating new body of knowledge and research focuses on how adults prefer to learn and the variety of new ways to teach so that employees retain more and actually use what they've learned. I'd like to share some of the best new ideas and remind you that teaching is not a lost art, even though the regard for it is a lost tradition.

Know the difference between these two words.

The two words "information" and "communication" are often used interchangeably when discussing training, but they signify quite different things. Information is giving out; communication is getting *through*. Let's commit to informing less and communicating more.

What you know most matters least.

It could be argued that in business today what matters most is not what you know but what you don't know. Identifying what you don't know makes your company stronger than crowing about what you do know. As consultant Thornton May said in a recent magazine article, "The real source of competitive advantage in any organization is how it deals with the fact that the people inside it don't know everything they need to know." An obvious first step in gauging what skills are in place and which need to be learned is to require both new and existing employees to complete a "can-do" versus a "can't-do" self-assessment before any training session. Design your training–all of your training–to actively answer the two key questions on every trainee's mind:

"So What?" and "Who Cares?"

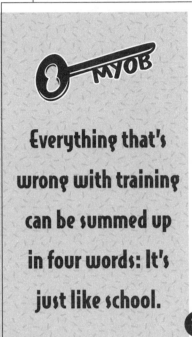

Everything that's wrong with training can be summed up in four words: It's just like school.

102

Where We Screwed Up With Training

The business world got screwed up in terms of training in the early 1970s when "experts" admonished employers to adopt a classic World War II training axiom: "Tell 'em what you're gonna tell 'em. Then tell 'em. Now tell 'em what you just told 'em." How many times have you heard a manager, supervisor or trainer use that phrase to explain how simple it is to train? But those knuckleheads never considered something even more important: how hard it is to *learn*.

Well, I say wake up, it's a New Millennium. That arrogant perspective–"Tell 'em, Tell 'em, Tell 'em–may have worked to "train" 18 to 29 year olds six decades ago, but that philosophy today is about as important as the foreword in a William Shatner novel.

Our employees and managers always will benefit from new skills, and the more we collectively educate our team, the better we collectively kick ass as a company. Your earnings depend on your learnings. We all have a huge stake in improving our people, performance, and productivity. So re-learn, re-think, and re-evaluate the traditional training process. Instead of deciding what information, policies, or processes we want the employee to learn and then designing a curriculum to go out and teach it, we're better off asking ourselves two basic questions:

- **How do our employees learn?**
- **What do they first need to unlearn?**

Effective trainers in the 21st century first must discover the existing knowledge base in their employees and then challenge it or change it, if necessary. Example: Let's say you run a restaurant and want to teach your servers to hand table tents listing your specialty drinks and desserts to

every guest when they first greet the table. Simple, right? So you gather the staff together, talk a little bit about what you're trying to accomplish, maybe show a video, explain what's in it for them, and then demonstrate the wrong and right way to use a table tent. You've followed the classic four steps of training: Tell, Show, Do, Review.

So, did you "train" them?
    Yep.
Are they using table tents now?
    Nope.

Why? Four reasons: First, we failed to focus on what current behavior they first had to unlearn. For example, they must first stop greeting a table with the phrase "You didn't want any desserts did you?" instead of handing the guest the dessert list as they enthusiastically recommend a specific choice: "the Heath bar crunch pie is incredible." Second, we failed to take into account that different people learn differently. Third, we assumed that a one-hour meeting about how to use point-of-sale merchandise would permanently change behavior. It won't. The fourth reason our trainees failed to use table tents is because *we imparted knowledge without context.* Let's look at the learning process in a little more detail.

Different Strokes for Different Folks

Just like the best service, the best training should be customized to the receiver, or trainee. Research scientists have argued for years about the many different ways adults learn. For instance, some people prefer to learn visually, others prefer hearing it, still others prefer learning kinesthetically (touching, handling). The most effective

"I don't know that there is another option to training people. As the world becomes more competitive we need to get more from our people by enriching their skills, you've got to take on the responsibility of training daily."

– Lawrence Bussidy, CEO, Allied Signal

learning involves a combination of all three. Of course, that's just one school of thought. Other studies break the learning process into much more detailed areas.

Here's a way of looking at learning along with a relevant exercise for you and your team members to use to help each person discover his or her preferred learning style. Let's assume that you just purchased a new computer. How would you react after opening the boxes? Sheila Udall in *The Accidental Manager*, suggests that an *Activist* prefers to learn by doing, so he most likely would set up the computer out of box and begin playing with it. A *Reflector* is someone who likes to think about and learn from experience, so before turning on the new PC, she thinks about how she used computers before. A *Theorist* prefers to understand the theory of how something works by reading and researching. So naturally he pores over the companion instruction manual first. A *Pragmatist* wants to know what something can do for you—its practical application—so she will review the table of contents and go to the sections that apply most directly to what she wants to use the computer for.

It's one thing to realize that the people you teach learn differently. It's another thing to realize that how you teach them may be contrary to how they learn. Trainer Lori Cross-Schotten points out that not only do trainees have a preferred learning style, but most instructors also tend to "train" in the same style in which they personally prefer learning. (Which may or may not resonate with trainees if their preferred learning style differs from that of the teacher.) Trainers should use a multi-media approach at even the smallest training sessions or meetings: appealing visuals, energetic delivery, video if appropriate. Approach training sessions like you're an ad agency doing a

presentation to land a large account. Attack all the senses, be clear, concise, respectful of the audience.
Be enthusiastic.

Learning Hasn't Taken Place Until Behavior Changes

Learning–or training–is a process, not an event. For example, if I talk to my son or daughter only once a year about being good, I won't get a good response. But constant communication and feedback ensure that my children can and probably will do better.

Or compare an hour-long tennis lesson every week for five weeks with five consecutive hours of tennis lessons. Which would make you a better tennis player? Most people would say the spread-out tennis lessons would be more effective than five consecutive hours. The same is true for most training. Training sessions should be conducted in segments, usually once a week. That way team members have an opportunity between sessions to practice the skills they are learning and receive feedback. (Adapted from *Shogun Management*, Wm C Byham.)

The best way to change behavior and impart knowledge is by committing to preshift team meetings every day. These brief preshift pep rallies should be timed–I recommend three minutes in length, maximum–and should focus on shift goals, highlight any potential problem areas, recognize recent outstanding performance, and promote the sales and service potentials of the next eight to 10 hours.

Here's a brief outline, and you can e-mail me at myob@execpc.com and I'll send you a free comprehensive list of how to conduct inspired pre-shift meetings.

The Five Steps of an Effective Pre-shift Team Meeting:

❶ **Market the Shift** (promote opportunities and customer traffic)

❷ **Dialogues, Not Monologues** (manager should speak 20% of the time, staff should speak 80%)

❸ **Play "I Say/You Say" (to foster interactivity)**

❹ **Set Goals for Each Shift**

❺ **Recognize and Reward Results**

106

Zeal without knowledge is like fire without light.

Context is key to making new behavior habitual. Understanding the knowledge and then knowing how to use it is powerful. When people understand what they're doing, they tend to do it better. For instance, any discussion of the importance of using table tents or brand names to sell more desserts had better be preceded by a lively education on how the price of an entrée barely covers the restaurant's fixed daily operating costs. "We must sell an entrée to generate gross sales. We must sell an appetizer or dessert to generate gross profit."

You don't just slap a "training veneer" over old habits and expect the new behavior to shine through. Unlearn first, detail the new behavior, present it in context to the P&L, and then learn and practice the new skill.

TEN COMMITMENTS OF LEARNING

Eye appeal precedes mind appeal. Are your training materials vibrant, exciting, reflective of the "fun place" you're promising they'll work in? Make sure your training manuals look more like *USA Today* than *The Wall Street Journal* in terms of layout, text, and graphics. Eye appeal precedes mind appeal.

Know the 90/20/7 Rule. Studies reported in *Training* magazine show that adult learners can listen with understanding for 90 minutes and listen with retention for 20 minutes. I agree, and I also suggest that you change focus or topics every seven minutes during your presentation in order to re-engage your audience to the subject matter. Where did I get this pearl of wisdom? Harvard Business School? No. Network television. They put commercials on every seven minutes to re-engage you when your attention begins wandering from the show. (And who said television can't be instructive?) According to another study, the average American high school student spends 14,000 hours in class and 19,000 hours watching TV. Yow! So adapt your training to the adult learner's bigger sphere of influence.

Use the K.F.D. principle when teaching adults. Before any presentation or training session, the group leader or facilitator should ask themselves three key questions: What do I want my audience to *know* about the subject matter? Then, how do I want them to *feel* about it? (Excited? Dissatisfied with current

TEN COMMITMENTS OF LEARNING

MYOB

The only thing that truly makes knowledge useful is the ability to grab it, use it, and then dismiss it after you're done with it.

conditions?) Last, what do I want them to *do* as a result of what they've learned? In other words, what behavior has changed? How will we measure it? How will we know if they "got" it? Are they pickin' up what we're puttin' down?

4 Synergize the "trainee" with the learning process. Design the content with relevance, deliver the content with passion, define the content in terms of behavior. Excite the learner about the education process, demonstrate the importance of "unlearning" as a prerequisite to learning. Emphasize much less learning by heart and much more knowing where to go to get information since the only thing that truly makes knowledge useful is the ability to grab it, use it, and then dismiss it after you're done with it. Encourage trainees to reflect on how they learn. For example, have trainees think of–but not write down– something they do well. After a minute or two ask them to *write down* how they got so good at the task or activity. Reason: The exercise will help them understand that the most successful learning depends on practicing and trying. In other words, provide trainees fodder so they don't mutter. And keep it fun. What we learn with pleasure we never forget.

5 Each one, teach one. The future of business will not depend on the "haves" and "have-nots" but rather the "knows" and "know-nots." The business that puts a premium on what their employees learn and how well hey share that knowledge with other team members is the business that will win the most customers and crush the competition. Confidence is a foundation of service. If you want to improve self-confidence, you do it by training. Create a culture of craving learners an eager teachers.

6 Plan presentations from the audience's perspective.
When you're planning a training session, remember how you feel when you're a trainee. Manage the basics first: Make sure the audience's sight lines for the presentation are clear and keep the visuals (flip charts, overheads, slides, posters, notes) large and legible. The Trainers "Rule of Six" is helpful: a maximum of six words per line, no more than six lines per slide, page, or poster.

7 Promote discovery, don't lecture. "What you discover on your own is always more exciting than what someone else discovers for you," says consultant Terrence Rafferty. "It's like the difference between romantic love and an arranged marriage." If you want to improve sales, don't call your staff together at a meeting and proceed to outline "the 30 ways you're going to boost sales." Instead, have them break into small groups of five and list as many ways as they can to increase sales. The advantages are twofold: One, they'll probably come up with better ideas than you did; and two, they're probably more committed to executing the ideas they brainstormed since—as I mentioned earlier—people never argue with their own data. World War II U.S. General George S. Patton put it this way: "Never tell people how to do things. Tell them *what* to do, and they will surprise you with their ingenuity."

"If I had 6 hours to chop down a tree, I'd spend 4 hours sharpening the ax."

–Abraham Lincoln, 1859

109

TEN COMMITMENTS
OF LEARNING

Reach out and Teach Someone.

8 Go back to school. Shake up your training program. Stay current on new discoveries and innovations in the adult learning field. Visit local elementary schools, talk to grade school teachers, and discover new teaching methods they're using to inspire children. Adapt it to your in-house training program.

9 Have fun. Let's lighten up. The amount of learning we do is directly proportional to how much fun you have. Engaging trainees with fun, interactivity, and a dose of familiar context via TV game shows is a winning combination. Instead of "reviewing content" at the end of a meeting, how about creating trainee teams that compete in a game-show format? I've been using a pretty fun program called "Game Show Pro" for the last couple of years. It allows you to customize training programs based on popular TV game shows like the *Jeopardy*, *Family Feud*, and *Tic-Tac-Dough* formats. E-mail me at myob@execpc.com for information on the company.

10 If They Haven't Caught It, You Haven't Taught It
Tie your training to the bottom line, because if it don't make dollars, it don't make sense. Measure training's impact. Hold trainers responsible for relevant content and program design that focuses on how people learn, and make them accountable for delivery methods that maximize involvement and retention. Hold your managers responsible for both supporting and executing the training. Yes, training is good for morale, the organization, and good for the employee's future. But if it doesn't bring more money they will go somewhere else for work.

Learning improves profitability. Period. And obviously people are a company's most important asset. If you have an excellent product and mediocre people, your results will be mediocre. Training is your secret weapon, the one tool you always can use to beat the competition, whether you're David or Goliath. Training doesn't "cost." It pays.

I'm aware that training is not a sexy topic in our industry, like marketing or promotion. But every profit-building activity in our business is predicated first on the assumption that your people can execute the service, sales, marketing, cost control, and safety issues that determine your success or failure. And now how *well* will they execute? As much or as little as you train–er, develop–them to.

Invest in unlearning before you learn, give each new behavior a context relative to the big picture, and follow the suggestions detailed above. You'll see significantly better margins and higher market share. Learning should be an active, lively process, not merely a combo manual-video. Training is like fish. The longer it stays on the shelf, the less desirable it becomes. So use it or lose it. Shake up how you train, and invest in how people learn. Don't just "reach and hire;" teach and inspire.

Training tames turnover. What causes employee churn? Three things: Don't Know, Can't Do, or Don't Care. All of which can be resolved by caring for and educating your people. Every day. Those that insist on following the traditional school method of "tell-me-training" may just see their profitability shrink as small as the period that ends this sentence.

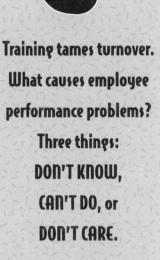

Training tames turnover. What causes employee performance problems? Three things: DON'T KNOW, CAN'T DO, or DON'T CARE.

"*A pat on the back is just a few vertebrae up from a kick in the ass.*"

–John Kucera,
Colorado philosopher

RECOGNITION, CONTESTS, AND REWARDS

Once your team is on a daily diet of knowledge and learning, the next step is to implement habitual recognition and intermittent rewards. Anything worth doing is worth measuring, and if you don't reward your best performers, the competition will.

A much ballyhooed 1991 study conducted by Dr. Gerald Graham from Wichita State University looked at 65 common workplace incentives. Here are the top five motivating techniques reported by employees, along with the percentage of times those techniques were actually used by their supervisors:

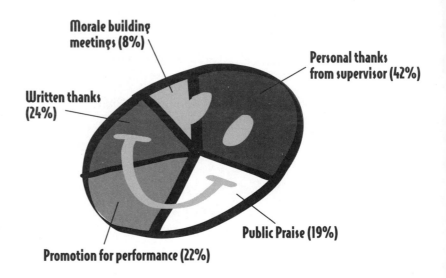

Morale building meetings (8%)

Personal thanks from supervisor (42%)

Written thanks (24%)

Public Praise (19%)

Promotion for performance (22%)

If those five factors are indeed as critical as our employees say they are, it seems to me that we've got five huge cost-effective strategies here to reduce turnover and build a more competitive team. So before you rush out and invest in an expensive incentive/merchandise catalog program to improve performance, remember that simple recognition and praise can go a long way to improve your productivity and profits.

A long time ago I jotted down what I considered to be the six key ingredients of a happy workforce:

- Appreciate us
- Involve us
- Develop us
- Lighten up
- Be flexible
- Create a "family" (Source: *The Motivational Manager*)

Also: never treat a customer better than an employee.

Service and Sales Contests

I personally have designed hundreds of effective employee contests and incentives for successful restaurant, supermarket, manufacturing, and department store chains in the last 20 years. The details of how to execute effective contests could fill up several books, and space limitations allow me to include only a handful of my favorites in this chapter.

If you'd like to share your best service, sales or cost control contest ideas with me, send them to me at myob@execpc.com, (or call (920) 830-3915) and I'll send you a list of contest guru's T.J. Schier's Top Ten Do's and Don't's for revenue-generating incentives in return. Plus, you'll be credited with your idea in a future edition of *Mind Your Own Business*.

Most of the contest ideas that follow are designed to encourage higher sales. If you're planning to implement sales contests, I have two suggestions. First, make sure that each contest is staged for no longer than 30 days. My experience has shown that hospitality employees tend to lose interest in contests lasting longer than a month.

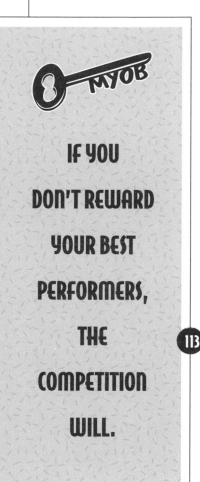

IF YOU DON'T REWARD YOUR BEST PERFORMERS, THE COMPETITION WILL.

113

Second, I strongly suggest setting team sales goals and never pitting individual sales people against one another. Let them compete against your other stores or other districts but not against each other unless they're in teams. It's OK to post individual sales records, but include that information as a subset of how the overall team is doing.

"20/20" Recognition Program: As particular performance criteria are achieved by individual employees, points are awarded, recorded, and added to other points earned. When an employee obtains a total of 20 points, a $20 gift certificate is presented to him/her, and the process begins again. This idea came from a supermarket operator who got it from a Harold Lloyd seminar. Examples:

Good Deed	# Pts.
Documented letter or call complimenting an employee	10
Detailed idea submitted in writing to improve the company	10
Six months perfect attendance (10 pts)	10
Birthday (2 pts)	2
Replace an employee who calls in sick (5 pts)	5
Recruit a person who eventually is selected (10 pts)	10
Successful mystery shop (10 pts)	10
Dean's list or honor roll (5 pts)	5
Department is accident free for 12 months (15 pts)	15
Community service participation (5 points)	5
Anniversary with company (5 pts)	5

Raffles: Go to a stationery or party store and purchase a package of raffle tickets. Every time an associate does something commendable, give him or her a ticket. The more tickets someone "earns," the better their chances of winning whatever it is you raffle off in a monthly prize drawing.

BYOB (Beat Your Own Best): Record the highest sales each employee has ever posted during a single shift. Now, have a contest to see who can exceed their personal bests.

The "Grand Slam" Order: This contest applies directly to tableside service restaurant operators, but it could easily be adapted to supermarket delis, too. Have a game that encourages servers to sell each customer a "Grand Slam" order. In the case of a tableside restaurant, that means a guest check that includes a beverage, an appetizer, an entrée, and a dessert. Each "Grand Slam" turned in receives a special raffle ticket. The more "Grand Slam Order" orders you sell, the better the odds of winning the raffle drawing at the end of the month.

Ticket Time Dollars: If you run a restaurant, you probably have specific cooking time goals set for every appetizer or entrée. And if takes too long to get that food out, service suffers. Here's an incentive that might help. Before a busy shift string 10 or 15 one-dollar bills on a wire behind the pass-through window. Tell the cooks that for every order that goes out beyond the target cooking time (measure by the time the ticket was fired), you'll remove a dollar bill. Whatever's left at the end of the shift is theirs to keep.

Sales Bingo: Create a bingo-style game board with at least 12 to 16 squares with a different menu item in each square. Servers who sell every item on the sheet or four in a row win a prize. Use fewer items and play Tic-Tac-Toe.

PASS THE BUCK

This idea is a restaurant classic. Pick items you want the waitstaff to sell, like a Cheddar Cheese Jalapeño Popper or Beer Battered Onion Rings. Give the server who sells the first appetizer a $5 bill. The server who then sells two appetizers takes the $5 bill from the server who sold the first one. The server who sells three appetizers takes the $5 from the server who sold two and so on until everybody is competing to sell more appetizers and one person finally owns the coveted $5. A variation of this is called "Pass the Envelope". The manager fills several envelopes with "surprise" prizes. On the front of the envelopes the manager writes the names of specific items they want to sell. First sale gets the envelope, second sale takes the envelope, etc...

 **Sales per Hour:** For deli team members who use a cash register to record sales or servers in a quick-service restaurant.

Highest Team Check Average: This contest works best for servers in a tableside restaurant. Measure the individual check averages of each server and bartender, and then break them into teams of three, cipher their collective check average, and encourage them to beat the other teams posted averages.

Group Weight Loss: Wellness programs that encourage healthy employee lifestyles, like weight loss, are beneficial to your business. A fun way to lose weight competitively without the embarrassment of individual weigh-ins is to get one department to challenge the others to see who can lose the most weight as a group. Team members of six to ten weigh-in on an industrial scale—available at local manufacturing plants—and see who safely can lose the most weight as a team over a prescribed period of time.

REWARDS

"All behavior is controlled by consequences; you get what you reward." –Author Bob Nelson

As far as rewards go, they say that cash is king, but savvy managers prefer merchandise. Cash is invisible. It disappears quickly into purchases, bills, or banks. Merchandise is tangible, visible, and has "brag value." I'm also a fan of awarding gift certificates to winners. Gift certificates can be cost-effective, too, if you trade out gift certificates from your business for gift certificates from other businesses. That way you're using "product dollars" and not real dollars. Avoid awarding gift certificates from your own establishment as prizes. Here are some creative ideas to consider:

Get Out of Work Free card. This incentive is self-explanatory; the contest reward is a card that allows the employee one day off (with a seven day advance notice).

Lotto Tickets. This is a great cost-effective way to reward exemplary performance at work. Each day buy five or six "quick-pick" Lotto tickets (not the scratch-off kind) and keep them in your pocket. You can use them for daily sales contest or to reward special service behavior or extra effort in the kitchen. What gets rewarded gets repeated.

Get rid of "employee-of-the-month" rewards. What's sadder than going into a restaurant or store on May 10th and seeing a plaque honoring the "employee of the month" that hasn't been updated since November? Forget "employee of the month." Celebrate "employee of the moment" every day, every shift, instead.

Commission Customized, Colorful pins: They can be worn on hats, shirts, or aprons commemorating special achievements like "ABCD" (Above and Beyond the Call of Duty) service, high sales, longevity, or recognition as a staff trainer.

Choose Your Own Schedule. Reward winners by allowing them to pick their work schedule for the next 30 days.

Good to See You in the News. Once a year take out a full page ad in the local paper thanking your employees by name.

"Well" Pay. In a large regional California restaurant company, employees get no sick days. Instead, they receive monthly well pay, equal to eight hours wages, provided they have been neither absent nor tardy.

Retro Safety Pay. If your team is working safer, consider dividing the money you save among the employees when workers compensation premiums go down due to reduced accident rates.

Spread the News. Feature the accomplishments of an outstanding employee in a news release and send it to trade publications or the local paper.

Staff Chooses. Employees won't push themselves to get rewards they don't value. Always get their input on the kind of prizes they'd work to achieve.

Special Parking spots. Award winners with the gift of a shorter walk than their teammates.

Scratch-off Cards or Pull Tab Game Pieces. These can be custom made for employees to support seasonal promotions, sales contests, service behavior or limited time offers (LTOs) in your operation. For more information on companies that specialize in those kinds of promotions, contact me at myob@execpc.com.

Use Cash as a Gift Wrap. Use dollar bills for wrapping pens, paper clips, coffee mugs.

Find Out Everyone's Dream. While not an actual prize, the concept means that managers take the time to know their employees better. Talk to them about their hopes and aspirations for the future, whether it's in your chosen profession or not. Know their spouses and children's names.

Handwritten Notes to Associate and Family. Never underestimate the power of a handwritten note or card sent to the employee's home recognizing the contribution the family or significant other gives to your success.

Bundle Pay with Thank Yous. Managers should always distribute paychecks personally to each team member and thank each associate individually. Don't forget to add the words "From Our Customers" on each pay envelope.

"Fraction of the Action." Outback Steakhouses has taken a leadership role in showing manager appreciation. The chain is open only for dinner, which reduces shift length, and the company allows managers actually to buy into the units in which they work. That gives them an obvious investment in that particular unit's success. Managers also can remain for at least five years at the same unit, hoping to contribute to a sense of ownership.

Give the Gift of Time. Olive Garden Restaurants converted from a three-manager system to a five-manager system to allow a 50-hour week with two days off. At the Cheesecake Factory, managers get two days off in a row, every week, just like a "real job."

Ten Pennies. Last, but not least, employee recognition– catching people doing something right–is a philosophy, not a department. If you're not in the habit of acknowledging your employees regularly and with enthusiasm, here's an effective technique that can help you change your behavior. Every morning put 10 pennies in your left pocket. Every time you praise a co-worker or call a manager to compliment a recent achievement, move a penny to your right-hand pocket. If you have any pennies in your left-hand pocket at the end of the day, you hurt the company, pure and simple. Success and pride begins with teaching everyone we work with the fact that what we do, large or small, matters.

It's the small things that can make a big difference. Be energetic, be enthusiastic, and always take care of your people.

SERVANT LEADERSHIP

"*They say that unless you're the lead dog, the view never changes. What they don't tell you, however, is that if you were a dog, you would probably prefer that view.*"
—Tim Cole, Kentucky gentleman

In the first sentence in this book, I pointed out that 3,000 business books are published annually in the United States. And based on highly un-scientific polling, I've come to the conclusion that roughly 2,995 of those books focus on the concept of leadership "secrets." The remaining five titles, incidentally, feature Chicken Soup, Habits, or Tae-Bo and the New Cardiac Kickbox CEO. So, I'm naturally a bit reticent to chew on a topic that's been beaten to death, routinely resurrected, and then pummeled back to the crypt again. So, rather than subject you to a didactic diatribe about the musings of Abraham Lincoln, Churchill, Martin Luther King, Napoleon, Chief Seneca, Lewis and Clark, and blah blah blah, I thought I'd instead share a few brief thoughts and personal nuggets on the key characteristics of effective leaders. What's the difference between a leader and a manager? Some say that a leader knows what's best to do, a manager knows how best to do it. And maybe the bottom line is this: the most important thing about leadership is what your people do when you're not there.

Passion and Purpose

"Talent is the gift plus the passion–a desire so intense that no force on earth can stop it."–Neil Simon, playwright.

A recent ad in a hospitality trade journal said it all: What did you make at work today?

- A tough decision?
- A happy customer?
- A paycheck?
- A difference?

A leader's job is about leverage: Leveraging inspiration. Passion. Purpose. People come to work to win. A leader understands that his or her primary role is to give everyone the tools and motivation to win.

So, how much do your employees value you as a leader? Answer this question honestly, and you'll know: When employees see you coming, do they say, "Here comes help," or "Here comes trouble?"

The bottom line is that you are the manager–or leader– that your people say you are. Their perceptions are your reality. Here are two simple steps you can take to establish yourself as a servant leader–one who has his head in the game, his heart on the line, and plays to win–in the eyes of your people:

- **Know, understand, and respect the role that each employee plays in the success of your business every day.** Never sell others short, and never overestimate your own value.

- **Be a thermostat, not a thermometer.** A thermostat has a steady reading and controls the temperature. A thermometer merely records the temperature, and can fluctuate wildly. Control your "temperature"

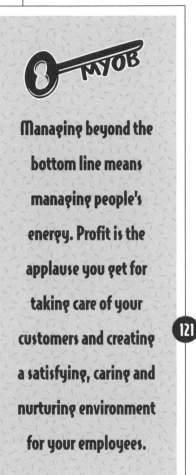

MYOB

Managing beyond the bottom line means managing people's energy. Profit is the applause you get for taking care of your customers and creating a satisfying, caring and nurturing environment for your employees.

when involved in discussions with customers and teammates. Nobody enjoys–or trusts–working for the "hot and cold" boss.

Credibility and Integrity

"About the only authority you hold today as a manager is the authority of your passion for the truth and your integrity," says one hospitality manager who prefers to remain anonymous. "The 'sticks' are pretty much gone. The 'carrots' are not what they used to be. Loyalty to the organization *per se* is pretty much gone. Your best hope is your credibility with your people."

Nuff said.

Remember: One lie does not cost one truth, but the truth.

Know that Questions are as Powerful as Answers

"Having all the answers isn't what makes a person a good leader–it's having a powerful inclination to ask questions," says Jerry Kaplan in his book *Startup*. "Why do we do something that way? Why do we do it at all? What if we did it this way? Why do I want to own (or run) this business? To ask *how* is get somebody else's answer; to ask *why* or *what if* is to seek your own." Good advice. Ask those first three questions of every process.

Share Information

Information Is Power? To me that is one of the biggest and most dangerous myths in business. It encourages people to hoard information–to use it as a weapon against

The speed of the leader determines the rate of the pack.
If you cannot win, make the person in front of you set the record.

122

colleagues (or customers) rather than as a way to solve problems. According to *Fast Company*, "The more people understand what's really going on in their companies, the more eager they are to help solve its problems."

Information isn't power. It's a burden. Share information and you share the burdens of leadership as well.

Put Team Before Self

"He climbs highest who helps another up."
—George Mathew Adams

It's your employees' job to take care of your customers. It's your job to take care of your employees. Having differences of opinion on your team is normal and healthy. But allowing those differences to divide a team or impede progress toward the collective company goal is deadly. As William Pollard said: "Diversity without unity makes about as much sense as dishing up flour, sugar, water, eggs, shortening, and baking powder on a plate and calling it a cake." We must stand united to beat the twin enemies of competition and inertia. To help you illustrate the importance of teamwork at your next meeting, try this exercise: Put a bunch of sticks in a bundle and have each team member try to break them. None will. Now, hand out one stick to each person and ask them to break it in half. It's easy. The moral? As long as you remain united, you are a match for all your competitors, but differ and separate, and you are undone. Root out and destroy bureaucracy and turfism at your business. And don't forget that *all work is teamwork*.

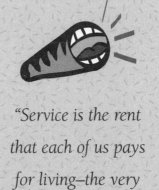

"Service is the rent that each of us pays for living–the very purpose of life and not something you do in your spare time or after you have reached your personal goals."

– Marian Wright Edelman

> "Yes, risk-taking is inherently failure-prone. Otherwise, it would be called sure-thing-taking."
>
> — Thomas Edison

124

Inspire a Collective Vision.

"Vision is what some people claim they have when they find out they guessed correctly."–Alfred E. Neuman in *Mad* magazine

In the early '90s, Honda Motor Company issued a corporate sales goal that–at first glance–was considered by many to be strange: "Six Hondas in Every Garage by the Year 2000." The company's leaders were trying to get its workforce and salesforce to focus on the breadth of the Honda line–motorcycles, generators, lawn mowers, snowthrowers, air compressors, farm equipment–as well as their best-selling line of automobiles. How crystal clear was their goal? Very. How sharply focused and easy to see is your company's vision ?

If you or your company are having a hard time with the "vision thing," I suggest that you, your managers, and teammates write out the answers to three simple questions:

If our operation were ideal, what would it look like?

How would we know when we got there?

What kind of training is necessary to achieve that ideal?

Work your way through this simple little exercise. Your goal is to be as specific as possible and detail the expected behavior as clearly as you can. I personally prefer the Collective Vision Statement to any Corporate Mission Statement. Let's go through sample answers of each question. I'll use the example of how I might respond to those questions if I owned a casual theme restaurant:

❶ *"If our restaurant were ideal, what would it look like?"* Every minute we're open, people are waiting to be seated. The front doors are held open by a smiling hostess for each entering or exiting guest and they are greeted or thanked by name. Each guest orders an appetizer that was suggested by a server, and a bottle of wine is on every table. Each entrée is prepared perfectly and the manager, servers, and bartenders know, use, and remember every guest's name. Servers recommend–and every guest orders–a dessert. After dinner, each guest orders a liqueur or dessert wine. Within 24 hours of visiting us, each guest is on the phone, fax, or e-mail telling at least two friends that they must come to our restaurant to experience the best service and food in the city. Those friends call two more friends each and invite them to lunch or dinner the next day at our place.

❷ *"How would you know when you got there?"* Obviously, all of the behavior you detailed in answering question number one would be happening. That's the importance of a clear, imagery-filled vision. You must communicate your vision clearly enough ("Six Hondas in Every Garage by 2000") so that each team member can clearly picture the finish line and how to get there. An old story illustrates the point very well: two workers were crushing rock at a construction site. Each was asked "What are you doing? The first replied: "I'm crushing rocks." The other replied: "I'm helping build a cathedral." Communicate your goals in a way that every manager and front-line service person clearly sees their role in building the business and, most important, serving the customer. Once again, it's a training and inspiration issue.

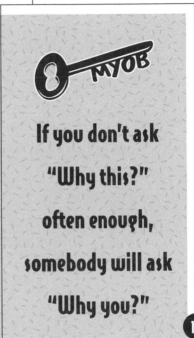

If you don't ask "Why this?" often enough, somebody will ask "Why you?"

❸ *"What kind of training is necessary to get you there?"* That question is easiest to answer but hardest to execute. Take a long look at how you answered question number one of this exercise, and then detail what kind of training you need to get your team demonstrating the behavior that characterizes the ideal operation. The point is that attaining a shared vision is not an esoteric exercise. There is a direct link between providing effective training and achieving corporate goals. The bridge between vision and reality is constant training, obsessive commitment to skills improvement, and providing team respect, recognition, and rewards.

Be CrazyUnorthodoxNuts

"Out on the edge you see all kinds of things you can't see from the center." -Kurt Vonnegut

Organizations, like people, hit "the wall." As a result employees lose energy, the company loses focus, and the competition gains customers.

Antidote? As consultant Pat Lynch says, "Don't think outside the box...blow the box up!" Challenge the process to get new perspectives. As I suggested earlier, don't just ask, "How do we improve this?" First ask, "Why do we do this?" If you don't take a chance, you don't stand a chance. Why *not* upset the apple cart? If you don't the apples will rot anyway. It's not as hard as you think. Innovation most of the time is simply taking A, B, C, and D, which already exist, and putting them together in a form called E.

Change is inevitable. Except from a vending machine.

"It's easy to come up with ideas; the hard part is letting go of what worked for you two years ago, but will soon be out of date."

– Roger von Oech, Writer

126

Commit to Serve Something Greater: **B A L A N C E**

Success and freedom are the
cornerstones of the leader's foundation.
Success is not what you own or what you're called. It's who you
are. Freedom is the act of serving something greater. We've all
heard the old phrase that no one on their deathbed ever
regretted not having spent more time at work. It's true. And
while the majority of this book focuses on ways to improve the
quality of work, it's more important to discuss ways to improve
our quality of life. Tend to your business, certainly. But tend to
your heart and soul, too.

I'm here to teach, not preach, and I know that the last thing
most people want in a business book is a sermonette about
the "soft stuff" of life. But we do work to live—most of us
anyway—not the other way around. So here are a few
reminders about the more important things.

- **The full life is the goal.** Yesterday is history; tomorrow
  is mystery; today is a gift—that's why we call it the
  present. Be here now. For your families, your
  customers, your teammates.

- **Give generously and strategically.** Good business
  people support both the community's and society's
  needs. As part of its business plan, a company has to
  consider the impact it has on society, relative to the
  environment, equal opportunity, work/family
  relationships, and community involvement. Invest in
  charities or community programs that make the
  most sense to your business's overall strategy and
  goals. When done right, a company's generous acts
  benefit not only the community and society but the
  company, too.

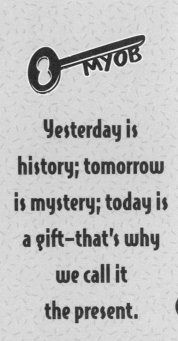

**Yesterday is
history; tomorrow
is mystery; today is
a gift—that's why
we call it
the present.**

127

Rethink opportunities for team building and spending. For instance, instead of an annual sales meeting, would your employees build a children's playground together achieve a bigger goal? When you help another, both are stronger. A story attributed to Martin Luther King, Jr., says it best: Two merchants were on a dangerous road and came across a man needing help. The first merchant asked, "What will happen to me if I stop to help?" The second merchant asked, "What will happen to him if I do *not* stop?" Remember, you get more than you give when you give more than you get.'

- **Go home and be with your families.** The things that count most in life are the things that can't be counted. One of the best perspectives I've seen on the subject of family priorities came from a Des Moines-area supermarket manager who had a handwritten sign over his desk. It said: "A hundred years from now it won't matter what kind of house I lived in, what kind of car I drove, or how much money I had in the bank. But the world could be different because I was important in the life of a child." What we must decide is how we are valuable rather than how valuable we are. Take good care of your kids. (After all, these are the people who will decide the quality of the nursing home you'll go into!) Don't fall into the possessions trap of working so hard to accumulate things that you end up missing the precious moments of your family's lives. Don't spoil what you have by desiring what you don't have. Remember that what you now have was once the things you hoped for. Don't forget: He who dies with the most toys...dies.

MYOB

Don't forget: He who dies with the most toys...dies.

In a recent conversation with Ken Blanchard, he stressed the importance of making the distinction between earthly success and spiritual significance. "Earthly success is about wealth, power, and status," he said. "Spiritual leadership is about generosity. Every day we should ask ourselves how can I make a difference?"

Dance Like No One's Watching.

A friend sent me the following story over the net. He had no source for it, and I've not been able to credit the author. But it rings so true that I thought that MYOB readers would appreciate it's perspective.

–Jim

"**W**e convince ourselves that life will be better after we get married, have a baby, then another. Then we are frustrated that the kids aren't old enough and we'll be more content when they are. After that, we're frustrated that we have teenagers to deal with. We will certainly be happy when they are out of that stage. We tell ourselves that our life will be complete when we get a nicer car, are able to go on a nice vacation, when we retire. The truth is, there's no better time to be happy than right now. If not now, when?

Your life will always be filled with challenges. It's best to admit this to yourself and decide to be happy anyway. One of my favorite quotes comes from Alfred D. Souza. He said, For a long time it had seemed to me that life was about to begin – real life. But there was always some

"Each of us will one day be judged by our standard of life, Not by our standard of living;
By our measure of giving, Not by our measure of wealth;
By our simple goodness, Not by our seeming greatness."

–William Arthur Ward

129

obstacle in the way, something to be gotten through first, some unfinished business, time still to be served, or a debt to be paid. Then life would begin. At last it dawned on me that these obstacles were my life.

This perspective has helped me to see that there is no way to happiness. Happiness *is* the way. So, treasure every moment that you have and treasure it more because you shared it with someone special, special enough to spend your time…and remember that time waits for no one.

So, stop waiting until you finish school, until you go back to school, until you lose ten pounds, until you gain ten pounds, until you have kids, until your kids leave the house, until you start work, until you retire, until you get married, until you get divorced, until Friday night, until Sunday morning, until you get a new car or home, until your car or home is paid off, until spring, until summer, until fall, until winter, until you are off welfare, until the first or the fifteenth, until your song comes on, until you've had a drink, until you've sobered up, until you die, until you are born again to decide that there is no better time than *right now* to be happy.

Happiness is the journey, not a destination.

Thought for the day:
Work like you don't need money,
Love like you've never been hurt,
And dance like no one's watching."

BE HERE. NOW.

"Risk more than others think is safe. Care more than others think is wise. Dream more than others think is practical. Expect more than others think is possible."

–Cadet maxim,
U.S. Military Academy,
West Point, New York

130

EXECUTION

Three frogs sat on a log and one decided to jump off. How many frogs were left on the log?*

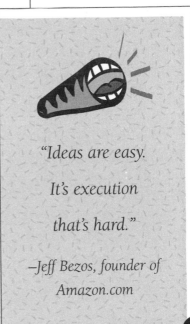

Whatever you know today is no guarantee you'll be successful tomorrow. To paraphrase *Future Perfect* author Stan Davis: The present instantaneously becomes the past, and business owners or operators with a "present" perspective always will be behind; to them, time is a constraint. For those with a future-perfect perspective, it's a resource; they've got time to get ready. If you are present-oriented only, you always must settle for catching up. The future is our friend.

A tired but true quote from hockey great Wayne Gretzky: "I skate to where the puck is going, not to where it is now." Or maybe Redd Foxx as television's Fred Sanford, said it better when he warned his friend Grady to "Change with the times, or the times'll change you." The minute you've "got business all figured out," business out-figures you.

So you've made it this far through the *Mind Your Own Business* philosophy and ideas. Now…whatcha gonna do? Well, my first suggestion is that you don't try to do everything at once, but *do something*. Circle, check, or

"Ideas are easy. It's execution that's hard."

—Jeff Bezos, founder of Amazon.com

131

* *Three. Moral of the story: There's a huge gap between what we decide to do and what we actually do.*

highlight the ideas you want to try first, then try *something*. My philosophy has always been one percent improvement in 500 things, rather than 500 percent improvement in one thing. My second suggestion is to beg you not to give your employees a "bath" with the ideas in this book.

Beware the Flea Dip Solution

When a dog gets fleas and you take it to the vet, you know what he does? He dips your dog into a flea bath and kills the fleas. But if your house still has fleas in the carpet, on the furniture, in the drapes–if you don't change the environment– the dog's just going to pick up fleas again. The same thing holds true for organizations. That's why so many potentially effective management theories from the 1980s and 1990s became "faddish" and ineffective. Good ideas get reduced to catch-phrases, and sloganeering replaces implementation. Execution is hard. Slogans are easy. Any employee will tell you that sloganeering is to improving performance what the Etch-a-Sketch is to art. There's no logical cause-and-effect. In order to become a MYOB-driven organization, we need to effect change in our entire culture. We need to inspire purpose and passion daily. We need to invest in employee education. Obsessively. Then, and most important, we need to get our people to take action.

MYOB

None of us is as smart as all of us.

Here are the three Most Important Questions of Your Next 12 Months. Rob Gilbert, in the newsletter *Bits and Pieces*, suggests that you can get people to take action by getting them to consider these three questions:

❶ What's the best thing that could happen to me, my family, or my company this year?

❷ What's the worst thing?

❸ What can I do right now to make sure that the best thing happens and the worst thing doesn't?

It is an extremely enlightening and fulfilling exercise to fill out the answers to those questions as soon as you can. Your responses will speak volumes about what to do and how to do it. At the same time, you'll see clearly both the direction signs and a road map of where you're going and what you'll need to get you there. A successful life and a successful business is all about taking charge. As poet Maya Angelou says, "Life loves being taken by the lapel and told, 'I'm with you, kid. Let's go.' "

Well done is better than well said.

They say that unsolicited advice is the junk mail of life, but I hope you will use what you've read here. It's irrelevant if you agree with my point-of-view or not. What you apply from this book is much more important than what you agree with. Acting on a good idea is better than just having a good idea. Try to be a finisher in a society of starters, and never be satisfied that you've done enough for your employees or your customers. After all, what is unexpected today will be expected tomorrow. Try to be better than your competitors or predecessors, but most important, try to be better than yourself.

Invest first in People, second in your Brand, third in bricks and mortar.

133

In this day and age of owners and operators touting terms like purchase cycles, marginalism, quantitative tools, usage yield versus functionality, shareholder linkage, and vertical integration, it's tempting–and easy–to relegate the customer or employee to a statistic or line item on a P&L. But when the meetings are over and the reports are all in, a simple fact remains: Despite what you may have heard, it's still a people business. Successful companies don't build business, they build people. People build business.

Show more interest in making the lives of each customer and team member happier and stress-free, and you won't have to spend as much time worrying about the bottom line or the stock market. Value the asset of *chispa*–"electric hospitality"–as a competitive tool. Hospitality is a powerful emotional energizer; it both doubles our joy and divides our sorrow.

While this book can provide a lot of direction, experience is still your best teacher. The irony, of course, is that experience is what prevents us from making the same mistakes over and over again. I call it *Deja Fu* ... the feeling that somehow, somewhere you've been kicked in the head like this before. And the only way to get experience is to make mistakes. So, the message to me is: Hey, if you're not failing, you're not trying. Add to your experience by implementing as many ideas in this book as you can. Then adapt, innovate, and improve on them. Choose your attitude, choose your behavior.

CHOOSE:

To be energetic every day for your team and your customer.

CUSTOMER LOYALTY OVER CUSTOMER SATISFACTION.

TO BE BRAVE. If you can take the worst, take the risk.

To first be the **BEST,** and then to be the first.

To teach **EACH EMPLOYEE** something new every day.

To be **HEALTHY.**

TO LIGHT THE WAY WITH A BLOWTORCH, NOT A CANDLE.

To beat the **PANTS** off the competition.

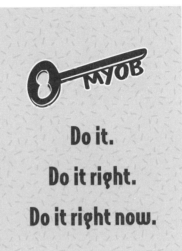

Do it.

Do it right.

Do it right now.

Be bold, not meek in battle. The race does not always go to the swift and the battle to the strong, but that's the way to bet. Always play to win. As my friend and esteemed colleague Tony Hughes of Bass Leisure Retail Ltd., says: "Make dust or eat dust."

Kick derriere.

In conclusion, I want to say that while the ideas in this book will improve your people, performance, and profits, I do not have all the answers on how to make your business thrive. Nobody has all the answers. (Which, of course, explains why you never see a headline that reads, "Psychic Wins Lotto.") And if you *do* believe that the future is predictable, you're either living in a dream world or your parents own the company. Will all the ideas in this book work? Well, the only thing I can say for certain is that *what isn't tried won't work.* And that's a fact, Jack.

So, add it all up, and what does it all add up to? The irony is that nobody knows for sure. In the long run, we can only do our best every day, have fun, love and respect one another as best we can, and hope to understand it all later. After all, business, like life, is experienced forward and understood backward.

This much is certain: Only you can make it happen. "Hope" is not a strategy. Now is the time, this is the place, and you are the person. This is your rocket. Let's ride.

THE END OF THE BEGINNING

"I always remember an epitaph I saw in the cemetery at Tombstone, Arizona. It says: 'Here lies Jack Williams. He done his damnedest.' I think that is the greatest epitaph a man can have."

–Harry S. Truman

136

THE FINAL TAKEAWAY:

Keep it fresh.

Keep it focused.

Remember to say thank you.

"Tools left in the toolbox never built anything."

MYOB Website

Now that you've read the *Mind Your Own Business* philosophy, why not transform the philosophy and ideas into action throughout your entire organization? It all begins at the *Mind Your Own Business* website. Start there and access dozens of new ways to improve your people, performance, and profits. To visit the *Mind Your Own Business* home page, just keystroke **www.sullivision.com**.

The site features a wealth of new and creative tips, tricks, and techniques every week on marketing, sales, service, rewards, and training that you can access free. Also, you can share ideas with your fellow hospitality professionals and get more information on MYOB live seminars, newsletters, CDs, audiotapes, and videos.

Have a great idea you'd like to share? Leave it. Have a great idea you'd like to borrow? Take it! It's free. Plus, you'll find links to additional sites and resources guaranteed to build your bottom line. See you there!

 And If you're just not in a cyberspace kind-of-mood, feel free to write me at:
Jim Sullivan - P.O. Box 2603 - Appleton, WI 54912

Phone/Fax: 920-830-3915
e-mail: myob@execpc.com

To order more copies of *Mind Your Own Business*, call our distributor at (800) 462-6420 or Lebhar-Friedman Books at (800) 453-2427 or visit our website at www.sullivision.com or the Lebhar-Friedman Books site at www.lfbooks.com.

FREE ELECTRONIC NEWSLETTER
If you'd like to receive the industry's number one monthly interactive idea exchange—The MYOB E-Newsletter, register at www.sullivision.com. It's FREE!

MYOB INDEX